GOLDEN RETRIEVER

SHEILA O'BRIEN SCHIMPF

Golden Retriever

Editors: Stephanie Fornino, Heather Russell-Revesz
Copy Editor: Joann Woy
Indexer: Dianne L. Schneider
Series Design: Mary Ann Kahn
Designer: Patricia Escabi

TFH Publications®
President/CEO: Glen S. Axelrod
Executive Vice President: Mark E. Johnson
Publisher: Christopher T. Reggio
Production Manager: Kathy Bontz

TFH Publications, Inc.®
One TFH Plaza
Third and Union Avenues
Neptune City, NJ 07753

Discovery Communications, Inc. Book Development Team: Marjorie
Kaplan, President and General Manager, Animal Planet Media / Kelly
Day, EVP and General Manager, Discovery Commerce / Elizabeth
Bakacs, Vice President, Licensing and Creative / JP Stoops, Director,
Licensing / Bridget Stoyko, Associate Art Director

Copyright © 2011 by TFH Publications, Inc.

Printed and bound in China

11 12 13 14 15 16   1 3 5 7 9 8 6 4 2

Library of Congress Cataloging-in-Publication Data
Schimpf, Sheila O'Brien.
  Golden retriever / Sheila O'Brien Schimpf.
     p. cm.
  Includes index.
  ISBN 978-0-7938-3721-2 (alk. paper)
  1. Golden retriever. I. Title.
   SF429.G63S343 2011
   636.752'7--dc22

                    2011009778

This book has been published with the intent to provide accurate and authoritative information in regard to the subject matter within. While every reasonable precaution has been taken in preparation of this book, the author and publisher expressly disclaim responsibility for any errors, omissions, or adverse effects arising from the use or application of the information contained herein. The techniques and suggestions are used at the reader's discretion and are not to be considered a substitute for veterinary care. If you suspect a medical problem consult your veterinarian.

Note: In the interest of concise writing, "he" is used when referring to puppies and dogs unless the text is specifically referring to females or males. "She" is used when referring to people. However, the information contained herein is equally applicable to both sexes.

The Leader In Responsible Animal Care for Over 50 Years!®
www.tfh.com

CONTENTS

ORIGINS OF YOUR
GOLDEN RETRIEVER

The Golden Retriever is a powerful hunting dog who can work all day in icy water and over uneven terrain to find a shot bird and bring it home, undamaged. Yet most people who live with Goldens will tell you—unasked—how sweet, biddable, and loving they are, with an uncanny ability to read minds. This seeming contradiction is the real strength of the Golden Retriever: He is master of many trades, friend to all, doer of great deeds, and strong and smart enough to make a difference in anyone's life. He is a sunny, funny, honey of a dog.

Today's Golden is one of the most popular breeds in the United States, still used for hunting but also excelling at agility, obedience, tracking, search and rescue, rally, therapy, and service dog work. All that and we haven't even mentioned how good looking he is!

THE GOLDEN RETRIEVER IN GREAT BRITAIN

Yellow dogs who look like big spaniels or setters appear in art going back at least 400 years. But it wasn't until the first Lord Tweedmouth, Sir Dudley Marjoribanks, bought a yellow dog in 1865 that the story of the Golden Retriever as we know it begins.

THE INFLUENCE OF LORD TWEEDMOUTH AND LORD ILCHESTER

Marjoribanks was a Member of Parliament who loved to hunt at Guisachan, his 20,000-acre estate in the Scottish Highlands. He hosted large hunts for his fellow aristocrats and kept various dogs, such as deerhounds and pointers, for the hunts. But hunting changed in the mid- to late-19th century. New guns made it possible for a single hunter to shoot more birds than he could before and to shoot them at greater distances. Hunting dogs had to change, and the Victorians were just the generation to do it. All over England at that time, dog breeders tinkered with dogs, breeding for longer legs or thicker hair or better noses, trying to produce the perfect dog for each job.

Marjoribanks had had much success breeding horses and cattle. He turned his expert eye to dogs and set up a large kennel on his estate with all the modern comforts and a large staff. In Brighton with his 16-year-old son in 1865, Marjoribanks was attracted to a yellow retriever walking with a cobbler. The dog had come from Lord Chichester's estate as payment for a debt, the cobbler said. He had been the only yellow dog in a litter of black Wavy-Coated Retrievers. Wavy-Coats carried the yellow gene and occasionally had a yellow puppy, known as a "sport," when recessive genes from each parent joined up. Marjoribanks bought the dog, named him Nous (Greek for "wisdom"), and sent him to Scotland

The Golden Retriever was developed to be a powerful hunting dog who can work all day in icy water.

for hunting. Several photos show Nous with great hunting parties—a large, solemn-faced dog resembling today's Golden Retriever. But Lord Tweedmouth wasn't done with him.

THE GOLDEN'S ANCESTORS

After a few years, Marjoribanks bred Nous to Belle, a Tweed Water Spaniel who came from the village of Ladykirk near the Tweed River. Golden Retrievers today come from two litters that Nous and Belle had in 1868 and 1872. From the first litter, three yellow puppies—Primrose, Cowslip, and Crocus—stayed at Guisachan. From the second litter, Ada went to live with Marjoribanks' cousin, Henry Edward Fox-Strangways, the fifth Lord Ilchester.

Marjoribanks kept kennel records that came to light in 1952; they detail many but not all of his breedings. But one thing is certain: The Golden Retriever was no accident. Marjoribanks developed the Golden over 20 years, breeding his yellow retrievers to another Tweed Water Spaniel, two black retrievers, a Red Setter, and probably a Bloodhound. The Bloodhound cross is not recorded in the records, but Lord Ilchester is said to have seen a note by Marjoribanks that had been stuck in the book he used for kennel records but lost. Marjoribanks also bred his dogs back to Ilchester's descendents of Ada.

Tweed Water Spaniels, one of the Golden's progenitors, were known for their excellent temperaments—a trait today's Golden still exhibit.

Lord Ilchester kept no records but said that he bred Ada several times to black retrievers. Yellow bitches such as Ada frequently had yellow puppies when bred to black dogs. Both men gave puppies to friends and neighbors, and soon yellow retrievers were working the fields around both their estates. Outside of Marjoribanks' select group, however, the yellow retrievers remained unknown. Black was the preferred color.

The black Wavy-Coated Retrievers who gave birth to Nous were a mix of setters who could retrieve and St. John's Newfoundlands, a smaller version of today's Newfoundlands. St. John's Newfoundlands were excellent swimmers, and their genes can be found in many retrieving breeds, including the Labrador Retriever, Flat-Coated Retriever, and Golden Retriever. English Water Spaniels and Collies were also part of the black Wavy-Coated Retriever background. (Black Wavy-Coated Retrievers evolved into today's Flat-Coated Retrievers.)

The Tweed Water Spaniel—Belle and other additions to Marjoribanks' Goldens—does not exist today. It had some similarities in size and looks to today's retriever and to the Irish Water Spaniel. The Tweed added yet another dog who was a strong swimmer and excellent retriever to the Golden's makeup. But the Tweed Water Spaniel was also known for its character traits, Rachel Page Elliott writes in an article posted on the Golden Retriever Club of America's (GRCA) website. Elliott, a well-known breeder and Golden Retriever historian, extensively researched Golden history and found that Tweed Water Spaniels had "qualities of unsurpassed intelligence and steadiness of temperament, combined with water prowess and willingness to work. To this fact all writers give testimony." She found a story of a Tweed Water Spaniel acting as a guide dog for a blind salmon fisherman, quoting the 19th-century dog writer, General W. N. Hutchinson: "Now this Tweed Spaniel was not born with more brains than other Tweed Spaniels, but he was [the blind man's] constant companion, and had, in consequence, acquired a singular facility of comprehending his order, and doubtless from great affection was very solicitous to please." Those traits could describe Goldens today.

THE GOLDEN'S ORIGINAL PURPOSE

Marjoribanks worked to develop a dog who could keep up with hunters armed with the newly improved shotguns in the hills and long grass of the Scottish Highlands. The guns picked up the pace of hunting and required a dog who could do more than point. The dogs had to wait patiently while the hunter found his birds. Then they had to tolerate the sound of a gunshot and keep track of where the birds fell. They had to go some distance from the hunter to find birds—lots of birds—in all weather and return them to the hunter without harming them. Birds frequently fell in water, so the dogs also had to be able to work in cold water.

THE GOLDEN TOUCH

Marjoribanks seems to have been attracted by the yellow color, but at first his dogs varied widely from pale to deep golden, almost red. Golden historians have suggested that he was at first more interested in improving traits such as swimming, a soft mouth (so as not to damage the bird), and nose before he moved on to color.

Marjoribanks' dogs were considered yellow retrievers, a variation on the black retrievers. Retrievers were interbred at first, as hunters sought dogs who were good at what they did—not what they looked like—and so all retrievers were in one class. Breeder Lewis Harcourt, who in 1904 acquired puppies from Marjoribanks' retrievers for his new Culham Kennel, started showing his dogs and preferred the name "Golden Retriever."

OFFICIAL RECOGNITION

By 1908, yellow retrievers began appearing in the relatively new world of dog shows—the Crufts dog show had started only in 1891. In 1909, Crufts had eight Goldens, and in 1910, ten. Then, in 1911, British breeders formed the Golden Retriever Club and wrote a standard. The Kennel Club officially recognized the

Golden Retriever in 1913, as the Golden or Yellow Retriever. The name "Yellow" was dropped around 1920.

Lord Harcourt's papers were donated to the Bodleian Library at Oxford University, including the Culham pedigrees. In about 1995, Golden historians began connecting the dots between Marjoribanks and Harcourt and found an unbroken line. Rose, from the last recorded litter at Guisachan, and puppies from a bitch whose mother was Lady, are behind the Culham dogs. The Guisachan dogs are the founding line of all Golden Retrievers.

THE GOLDEN RETRIEVER IN THE UNITED STATES

Goldens made an early, fleeting appearance in the United States before the turn of the 20th century. Marjoribanks' youngest son, Archie, went to Texas with one or more of the new yellow dogs to run a ranch between 1883 and 1893, according to Golden breeder and historian Marcia Schlehr. A dog named Sol was, in Marjoribanks' studbook, noted as "given to Archie, died at Ranche." Schlehr believes that Sol fathered Lady, who was born in Texas, possibly in the early 1890s. Archie later went to Canada to work for his brother-in-law, the governor general of Canada, and took Lady with him. In 1894, Archie was photographed with Lady, a handsome-looking bitch with that same Golden look that today's dogs have. Although they were undoubtedly the first Goldens in North America, Sol and Lady left no record of any descendents in the United States. In England, however, Lady's grandpuppies were the foundation for Harcourt's famous Culham Kennel.

Goldens appeared in a few hunting photographs in the U.S. and Canada around the same time, and the assumption is that they were shipped to the U.S. from Britain by retired British military officers for hunting. It wasn't until well into the 20th century that Goldens gained a permanent foothold in North America, with the founding of two Canadian kennels. Bart Armstrong founded Gilnockie Kennel in Winnipeg, Canada, in 1922. Colonel Samuel S. Magoffin, an engineer, founded the Rockhaven Kennel in Vancouver, in 1932. Magoffin became one of the most important figures in North American Golden history, helping to establish the Golden as a widely accepted and admired hunting dog and family companion.

Lord Tweedmouth is the founder of the Golden Retriever breed.

MAGOFFIN'S LASTING INFLUENCE

It started in 1930, when Magoffin imported Speedwell Pluto, born in 1929, from Britain. Magoffin was looking for a hunting dog, and the Golden had been highly recommended. Pluto became the first Canadian champion and father of many famous Goldens, but he was first a hunting dog who was regularly working in the field. He set the pattern for all of Magoffin's dogs. Magoffin also imported two foundation bitches for Rockhaven, the sisters Saffron Chipmonk and Saffron Penelope.

When the American Kennel Club (AKC) registered the first Goldens in 1925, they were classified simply as retrievers, along with all other retrievers, and they were shown together. When the AKC recognized Goldens as a separate breed in 1932, they were entitled to compete separately for the first time, not with other retrievers, Schlehr says. Pluto became the first American AKC champion Golden in 1932, and he was the first Golden to win Best in Show, in 1933. His offspring include four American champions and many Canadian champions.

Magoffin inherited Gilnockie Kennel when Armstrong died, moved the kennel to Inglewood, Colorado, and put his brother John in charge. Magoffin also got his wife's two brothers and a sister (the Boalts) involved in Goldens, as well as two of their friends. Seven Golden kennels in three states—mostly in the upper Midwest—sprouted under Magoffin's umbrella.

Magoffin loved the dog he championed. In 1938, he wrote in a guest column in the *American Kennel Club Gazette*: "What we have in the Golden Retriever is a grand hunting dog for both upland game and waterfowl during the hunting season, and the best companion imaginable for all the family for the balance of the year."

THE GOLDEN RETRIEVER CLUB OF AMERICA (GRCA)

In 1938, the Magoffin brothers and other Golden breeders started the GRCA, incorporated in Colorado. Sam Magoffin was its first president. The first yearbook listed 43 members, and the first national specialty was held in Wisconsin, in 1940. Gilnockie and Rockhaven dogs were heavily represented in both shows and pedigrees for decades.

The GRCA has about 5,000 members, making it one of the largest breed clubs. It has a foundation for health research, a large national specialty event every year with educational seminars, and a sophisticated magazine, *The Golden Retriever News*. It promotes the Golden as a gundog and an all-around breed, and supports serious breeders who subscribe to its code of ethics. The code requires breeders to use only dogs tested for health of hips, hearts, eyes, and elbows.

A nationwide network of more than 50 local dog clubs also belongs to the GRCA.

The Golden Retriever Club of America was founded in 1938.

These clubs refer buyers to breeders, host local dog shows and field trials, stage educational seminars, and allow Golden owners a place to meet and learn from each other.

THE GOLDEN'S RISE IN POPULARITY

Both World War I and World War II slowed the growth and spread of Golden Retrievers in Great Britain and the United States. According to Schlehr, Ilchester's kennel closed during World War I.

GROWTH IN GREAT BRITAIN

In Great Britain, historian Elma Stonex writes that so few dogs were bred during World War II that those who were sold for high prices. Unscrupulous breeders jumped into the gap. Stonex writes that, for a few years at the end of the war and immediately after, these "breeders" produced a generation of Goldens that included dogs who were oversized, under-boned, and flat-footed. The number of Goldens registered by the Kennel Club barely rose from 1,073 in 1938 to 1,385 in 1945 but started steadily increasing by 1950. Goldens were the seventh most popular breed in Great Britain in 2008, with 9,159 registered.

Goldens gradually became lighter in color and heavier in appearance—less willowy and more compact.

GROWTH IN THE UNITED STATES

In the United States, throughout the 1930s, the Magoffins and the Boalts bred dogs in the Midwest for field work, and the Golden gained a reputation as a first-class hunting dog, perfectly suited to Midwestern terrain. They looked much like the British lines they were bred from. In other parts of the country, some breeders concentrated on show dogs rather than hunters. The Golden was still not widely known or available.

Throughout the 1940s and into the 1950s, many Goldens were tall and dark, with narrow heads. By 1950, Schlehr writes, some Goldens were almost 27 inches (68.5 cm) tall. (Today's breed standard calls for 23 to 24 inches [58.5 to 61 cm] for males.) The GRCA operated under the same standard used in England until 1955, when the club revised it to allow dogs to be disqualified for being too tall, for having incorrect bites, and for abnormal eyelashes. Few changes have been made since.

SHOW DOG VERSUS FIELD DOG

In these decades, the Golden was primarily a hunting dog but also was considered an all-around dog who could do anything. Schlehr proudly comments that many dogs at national specialties showed in conformation one day and ran field trials the next. But gradually show dog breeders and field dog breeders began to emphasize different things. They began to specialize.

By the 1970s, the rare yellow retrievers bred for the Scottish aristocracy had become a popular American family dog—even a status symbol. One named Liberty lived in the White House. By now they came in two looks: show and field. Show dogs were flashier, with heavier feathering on the legs and rear, and tended toward lighter coloring. Field dogs were sometimes darker, had higher energy and shorter coats, and were bred for their hunting ability rather than looks.

Something similar happened in Great Britain, where a distinctive style evolved after World War II. The English Golden—popular in Canada and in Europe—is bigger boned, heavier, and shorter, with a blockier head and wavier hair. And although they may be any color, some of them are a cream color not allowed in the American show ring. English breeders also specialize in field or show Goldens, Marcia Schlehr notes. "But many of the British field trial dogs are well structured and very typical in build, as their field trials have much less emphasis on speed and rigorous 'mechanical' handling, more emphasis on the dog's natural abilities such as working on their own to find the birds. In both countries, there are many 'show' line dogs who do still retain ample natural ability—they just don't often have the chance to develop it. Some of the British show lines are very pale in color, and the field working people don't much care for the very pale color." Underneath, though, all styles of Goldens share a passion for life, that Golden temperament, and a willingness to please.

HEALTH ISSUES

In both field and show dogs, health issues cropped up. As Goldens became popular, more people began breeding them, people who did not have the fine eye or long-term interest in the breed at heart. Line breeding to reproduce the look of a prize-winning champion sometimes became inbreeding, with all of its potential genetic faults. Hip dysplasia crept in, as well as other genetic defects that come from overbreeding—eye, heart, and immune system weaknesses. Cancer became a major cause of death.

The GRCA responded to these challenges, becoming the first breed club to write a letter that goes out with AKC registration papers for every Golden. The letter welcomes new Golden owners and then states several hard and fast truths: Goldens have a legendary desire to please that translates into a wish to be with people all the time. They need considerable exercise every day, proper vet care, excellent nutrition, and obedience training. They could potentially have serious genetic problems, including hip dysplasia, eye problems, epilepsy, skin allergies, and heart defects. Hips, eyes, and hearts should be tested before breeding any Golden, the GRCA warns.

The GRCA Advisory Council on hip dysplasia was an early voice against breeding dogs with hip dysplasia, Schlehr says. The GRCA began in the late 1950s to collect X-rays of hips, looking for early signs. This idea was adopted for all breeds in 1966, when the Orthopedic Foundation for Animals (OFA), a national registry, was founded. The OFA's website (www. offa.org) lists hip ratings and other types of clearances.

Field-style Golden usually have short coats and more en than the show-sty

THE GOLDEN RETRIEVER TODAY

Today, the Golden Retriever is fifth in popularity in the United States as measured by the number of AKC dog registrations, following the Labrador Retriever, German Shepherd Dog, Yorkshire Terrier, and Beagle. The Golden's sunny, loving temperament is renowned and has replaced hunting ability as the reason most people want a Golden.

Goldens are sensitive dogs who respond to a command as subtle as a gesture or a nod of the head. They are people lovers, craving human companionship, and are not suited for kennel or backyard life. They are tolerant of most children, especially those in their own house, and can be taught to accomplish a wide range of tasks, from dog sports to guide dog work. They do not make especially good guard dogs, although some will bark at a stranger at the door. After that, though, they will threaten the stranger with licking or beating with their tail. But they are still large, powerful animals who can withstand icy water, look longingly at a duck on a pond, and run all day with a tennis ball.

"You can do anything with them," says Gwen Coon of St. Johns, Michigan, whose twelve-and-a-half-year-old Golden 2Ts is a MACH 3 agility champion. "They are so willing."

CHARACTERISTICS
OF YOUR
GOLDEN RETRIEVER

olden Retrievers are big, hairy, beautiful dogs who like nothing better than to roll in a mud puddle and shake mud on the nearest person. They require owners who will spend time brushing them, vacuuming the house and car, and exercising them. It seems like a lot of work, right? So why do they have a regular place on the American Kennel Club's (AKC) list of most popular dogs in the United States? Because "golden" doesn't refer just to their color. These dogs have a temperament worth gold, most owners will tell you. Once you've had a "conversation" with a Golden, for example, other dogs just seem to fall short. They are tuned to your brain waves. And if you've ever been loved by a Golden, there's no going back. Goldens are good-natured, intelligent, versatile dogs who can match their owners' wildly differing expectations: couch potato, agility partner, rally companion, service dog, obedience champion, hunter, or—the most important—true friend.

PHYSICAL CHARACTERISTICS

The Golden should be, in a word, handsome. This eye-catching dog has style, power, coordination, and an alert, intelligent expression. He is beautiful to watch trotting, and breathtaking when he is in a full gallop or jumping hurdles. All of that beauty, though, should have a purpose. He should look like he is able in every way to retrieve a downed duck.

BODY

The Golden is an almost square, medium-sized dog with a double coat in any shade of gold and an expressive face that communicates easily to people. He has a substantial body, with solid bones, big feet, a hard-to-ignore tail, and thick neck—there is nothing fragile about him. He exudes physical energy; it is easy to imagine him racing over the Scottish Highlands, duck held softly in mouth, back to the hunter he loves. He should also project a gentle nature and likeability, drawing people closer to him rather than driving them away.

Neck

The Golden's neck should be medium long, and his back should be straight and level. But his back should not be long. In fact, the space between his last rib and his rear end should be very short. Most of the dog's body is rib cage.

Legs and Paws

A Golden should have strong legs, straight in some places and angled in others but never bowed in or out. The front legs should look straight to anyone

standing in front of the dog. From the side, the shoulders should show an angle resembling a sideways "V" above the legs. The rear legs should show more visible angulation from the side—the sideways "V" of the front plus an additional line that resembles a misshapen "Z." From the rear, a Golden's legs should be straight and parallel.

Goldens have large webbed paws. A Golden puppy has such large paws that sometimes people fear that he will grow to be a giant. In fact, he will become a medium-sized dog with large paws and some webbing between the toes to help him swim better.

The breed has round, compact feet with thick pads. The nails may be light or dark. The front feet may have a fifth nail, or dewclaw, above the foot that many breeders remove a few days after birth, but if your dog still has dewclaws, he will manage well. The dewclaws are removed to give the leg a straighter look, to reduce the number of nails that need to be cut, and to prevent them from catching on things. In reality, they rarely snag anything and occasionally come up with grass stains, showing that the dog uses them in a full gallop.

The legs and feet are designed to help the Golden run and swim. They absorb shock on land and help him paddle through ponds.

Tail

The Golden tail is a thing of beauty—a plume of airiness that actually serves as a strong rudder when he is swimming. The tail hair hides a strong, muscular tail that also assists with balance. The plume, frequently lighter colored than other parts of the body, also helps a hunter keep track of a dog in a dark reedy marsh.

SIZE

The Golden was designed to be big enough but not too big. Golden people talk about moderation and balance. Males should weigh between 65 and 75 pounds (29.5 and 34 kg) and females between 55 and 65 pounds (25 and 29.5 kg).

Golden height is measured at the withers, the highest point of the shoulder. Males should be 23 to 24 inches (58.5 or 61 cm) and females 21.5 to 22.5 inches (54.5 to 57 cm). In the dog show world, professionals are frequently seen using their fingers to measure dogs because the show standard asks that Goldens be slightly longer than tall, in a ratio of 12:11.

So how to account for all of the 90-pound (41-kg) Goldens who can countersurf without getting up on their hind legs? Some of it is breeding. Longer legs appeal to some people, and others just breed any two dogs they like regardless of height. Some people like big dogs and think the more Golden the better. Some of it is a shift toward stockier, bigger-boned dogs who carry an extra 1 or 2 pounds (.5 to 1 kg). Some of it is just owner indulgence—some think that if one cookie is good, two is better.

The standard has barely changed since the descendents of Lord Tweedmouth's dogs showed up at dog shows in the early 1900s. The Golden was meant to be a medium-sized dog, powerful enough to work all day in hilly country and able to swim in cold water carrying a heavy duck. They are also sized to fit in small boats, leap off, find the

The Golden's eyes should be brown—t darker the better.

A Golden in full coat is a dog of beauty.

duck and retrieve it, and be pulled back into a boat by a hunter. The super-sized Goldens don't match the earliest designs and probably couldn't do what they were meant to do.

HEAD

Goldens have a striking head, easily recognized in profile. The nose should be straight with a definite stop, the rise where the nose meets the forehead. The head itself should be broad, and the face should match. The flabby skin under the cheeks (flews) and chin should be minimal. His eyes should be brown, the darker the better, with dark black rims—mellow puddles that are easy to get lost in. The ears are shorter than those of spaniels and setters and should be level with his eyes. The dark pigment around the eyes should match the color of his nose, although the pinkish snow nose is acceptable in cold weather.

Teeth are very important in a hunting dog who has to pick up and carry game. The Golden should have 42 teeth and a scissors bite. This means that the outer side of his lower teeth should touch the inner side of his upper teeth. Even if your dog will never pick up a downed bird, the number of teeth and their alignment are important. Misaligned teeth that don't meet top and bottom when chewing, top teeth that either stick out over the bottom or fall behind the bottom teeth, and multiple missing teeth can make it hard for your dog to eat. They also make it difficult for dogs who have to pick up other things, such as service dogs who pick up keys and pens, and dogs in obedience competition who pick up dumbbells. Teeth are so important in Goldens—and early Golden breeders were so worried about mounting evidence of teeth problems—that the show dog standard allows judges to eliminate dogs with a bad bite or obvious gaps in their teeth. Only dogs with a scissors bite and all of their teeth should be bred.

BE AWARE!

Most Goldens are food motivated. Special treats can help persuade an exuberant young dog that sitting and waiting for you to open the door is worth it. And it may save his life some day.

COAT

A Golden in full coat is a dog of beauty. True to their Scottish Highlands origins, Goldens have a thick double coat to keep them warm while working outdoors in inclement weather. Close to the skin is a short thick coat, usually light cream in color, that insulates the dog from the elements. On top is a straight or curly coat of longer hair that is usually darker—a shade of gold—that repels water. This double-layered coat works on many levels. It keeps the dog warm in cold weather and cooler in warm weather, protects against sunburn, and resists rain and sleet. And it is part of the Golden look! A Golden with a thin coat and patchy growth might have a health issue and should be seen by a vet.

The Golden should have lighter-colored, longer hair on the legs, tail, and rear end, sometimes called "feathers," and longer hair around the neck in a ruff. The hair should be medium textured, not too silky or coarse.

Goldens shed this beautiful hair at least once a year. The coat, which should be brushed weekly or twice weekly, must be brushed daily during a shed. The coat is so thick that, when hair falls out, it frequently gets trapped between layers, creating a mat that has to be cut out. Brushing a dog who is shedding may not be enough to get through to the skin and grab all of the loose hair; a Greyhound comb with wide-set teeth is recommended.

COLORS

Goldens come in many shades of gold, from dark to creamy. Lately, the lighter shades are more popular. Goldens should, however, never be white or deep red like an Irish Setter.

"Color is so important," says top-winning handler and Golden breeder Amy Rodrigues Booth. "It's a part of their name. A Golden Retriever should not be white but gold."

The gold in the dog's hair usually picks up the sun and sparkles. Lord Tweedmouth may not be responsible for that, but many Golden lovers appreciate the glint.

LIVING WITH A GOLDEN (OR TWO)

New Golden owners are sometimes surprised by how strong their dog is, how soft his mouth is, and how he does not arrive on day one as the legendary "perfect family dog." Their reputation as the premier biddable companion may lead new dog owners astray. People who have dogs who read their minds, walk off leash, and companionably sit on the couch with them every night are people who have socialized their dogs, taught them manners, and poured time and energy into their education. Goldens can become the perfect dog, but it may take two or even three years of training and living with a family. They rarely come home from a breeder or rescue group ready to fulfill your deepest desires. They need to be fully mature (about three years old), well socialized, and engaged in household life before they become the dog in those Golden stories.

Properly socialized, Goldens get along wonderfully with children and other dogs.

COMPANIONABILITY

Goldens are social animals. They like people. They even like other dogs. They love other Goldens.

If you introduce your puppy to a wide variety of living creatures, he will learn to live with children, elderly people, other dogs, the neighbors' dogs, dogs at the dog park, and even cats. Occasionally, a Golden will try to defend you against a big dog he is afraid of.

You can usually take a Golden to a dog park or beach without worrying that he will attack a toy dog. They are normally good-natured with children they meet on their daily walks, and they see another human as someone who will shower them with the attention they crave. But each dog is unique; if a puppy has a bad experience with someone or something, he may never forget, and he will approach the next child or wheelchair or whatever frightened him with apprehension. Over time, you will learn how your dog reacts and be able to predict his behavior reliably (although there are no guarantees with squirrels and rabbits; Goldens will try to chase both—anywhere, anytime).

ENVIRONMENT

Goldens can do well in almost any environment: rural, suburban, or urban. But there are three things to remember: 1.) They need a generous amount of human companionship. 2.) They are big dogs. 3.) They need exercise every day.

But the most important thing, no matter where a Golden lives, is that he develop a relationship with at least one human. Goldens were designed to work closely with a human hunter, and they need that type of close relationship to be completely satisfied.

Rural

Rural folks have plenty of space for a big dog. Farms or ranches can be very good places for Goldens. In the country, Goldens will get enough exercise, but owners need to watch for dangers that come with less supervision, such as porcupine quills and skunk sprayings. They need to be sure that their dog learns to walk on a leash and gets enough time with his people.

Suburban

The suburban neighborhood may be the perfect setting for a Golden. A fenced yard that is available at any hour, in any weather is a boon for both dog and dog lover. Neighbors who like your dog can help expand his knowledge of people and let him out if you are away for a day. Also, the opportunity to take walks together around the neighborhood is a bonding experience for most dogs and owners and allows the Golden to use his nose.

Urban

People who live in a very small apartment and still want a Golden must develop a plan. It is not impossible—it just takes thought. Goldens

Dog Tale

Goldens are champion swimmers, but at first some need to be convinced of this. Our Dash played on the beach one whole day before I persuaded her to chase a tennis ball out into the lake where the water was over her head. Then we couldn't get her out of the water!

Goldens require a lot of exercise and a lot of different types of exercise.

living in small spaces need two walks a day in addition to the regular morning and late evening bathroom breaks. Dog walkers can be hired to help. Apartment-living Goldens need to visit a dog park or other safely fenced area several times a week so that they can chase a tennis ball off leash.

EXERCISE REQUIREMENTS

Goldens need a lot of exercise. Period. The only thing more to say is that they require different types of exercise. A tired Golden is a good Golden.

At a minimum, this breed needs at least one leash walk every day that covers 1 mile (1.5 km) or more. Once or twice a week, a 2- or 3-mile (3- or 5-km) walk is good. Rhonda Hovan, Golden breeder and Research Facilitator for the Golden Retriever Club of America (GRCA), recommends 3 miles (5 km) a day. This breed is happy outdoors even in the rain or snow, and watching that enthusiasm makes even a cold, wet walk more interesting.

Occasionally, Goldens need to run full-tilt off leash somewhere—in the backyard, a friend's yard, a dog park, or any fenced safe area. They can chase tennis balls, birds, or squirrels. Swimming is another good exercise option for Goldens.

Golden owners often keep a list of equivalents in their head. An hour of this equals 2 miles (3 km) of that. I can't walk today because of the ice or the cold, but I can stand in the backyard and throw a tennis ball for 20 minutes. We went to the dog park this morning, so I am only going to walk .5 mile (1 km) tonight. We went swimming yesterday, so we are taking a shorter walk today. The idea is to make sure that your Golden gets to stretch his legs every day and run with abandon two or three times a week.

EXUBERANCE

People who are attracted to a Golden frequently like his alert, intelligent look and enthusiasm. But sometimes they forget that he has the same 24-hour day they have. A one-hour walk/playtime while you savor his exuberance is only a small part of your dog's day. That same energy carries over into everything he does: greeting strangers at the door, jumping out of the car, racing up and down stairs, eating dinner, etc.

People who are socializing their Golden sometimes find that *wait, walk slow*, and even *leave it* can be difficult for their dog. This breed is impulsive by nature and wants to enthusiastically do everything *now*. But with time and patience on your part, he can learn.

Golden lovers like his alert, intelligent look and enthusiasm.

The Golden's exuberance is legendary and will cheer you up on a cold rainy day. But the flip side of that is that he will follow you around the house, enthusiastically asking for something to do, thrusting that big broad head into places you might wish he had never seen.

MOUTHINESS

Goldens were bred to bring home a duck without damaging it. This means that they have sensitive mouths, which they use like a fifth paw. Puppies, especially, learn by putting things in their mouths. If there are no ducks in your kitchen, your Golden may try for a dishtowel, a pair of dirty socks, a decorative pillow, a throw rug, or even the fleece you put in his crate. Goldens like to carry things in their mouths, and fabric things appeal to them, especially when they're puppies. A house with one or more Goldens should have several toys strewn across the floor so that they can pick up and carry something when they feel the need.

Puppies—and in particular Golden puppies—are extremely oral. They will do things like grab at a sleeve, and although they may rip it at first, will soon learn how to latch on to it without a tear. Very young puppies will also mouth your fingers. It is best to teach them not to grab at people with their mouths. (See Chapter 8 for information on how to teach your dog not to nip.)

All of this means that you must keep things off the floor that might end up in your dog's mouth. Magazines, newspapers, knickknacks, rattan baskets, tissue boxes, toys, and dirty clothes are the most obvious. But other things could also end up in your puppy's mouth—pills, coins, bobby pins and bands, even paper money that falls on the floor. Each puppy seems to have his own preferences, and until you know what your puppy's preferences are, it's best to clear the decks.

TRAINABILITY

Dog trainers and dog books frequently rate the Golden as highly trainable, and he is. The breed is successfully trained for highly complicated tasks such as service and guide dog work, search and rescue, drug detection, cadaver recovery, and obedience, rally, and agility competition.

But like anything else, the experts make it look easy. A smart dog like a Golden plopped into a busy family that is gone all day may soon be running the house. An untrained Golden will chew things (including wallpaper and the drywall underneath, wood trim around doors, throw rugs, and the legs of wood furniture), beg for food so much that people protect their plates at mealtime, jump on people constantly, use his mouth to grab arms to get attention, and hopelessly pull whenever anyone tries to put a leash on him.

The question with the highly trainable dog is who is training whom—is it you or the dog? The self-trained dog is hard to live with because his priorities will usually be different from yours. It is better to train him to do what you want him to do, and with a Golden, that usually means obedience classes. This extremely social breed will watch the other dogs and learn more quickly from them. Even the rare shy Golden will learn basic commands despite himself. A year or so later, if you say a word that was a command in the class, your dog will execute it flawlessly. Goldens absorb everything they see and hear, even if they do not immediately turn into an obedience champion. Training a dog is a process, not a one-time accomplishment.

Your Golden can learn quickly and is highly trainable—provided you give him the instruction he needs.

Goldens respond best to positive reinforcement, which includes treats and praise.

Goldens learn so quickly that multiple repetitions in one session may be too much. Repeating something such as "Shake" ten times in a row, for example, may drive both you and your dog to distraction and make training difficult. It is better to repeat a lesson two or three times, then move on to something else.

Goldens are considered "soft" by dog trainers—soft meaning sensitive. Using harsh training methods, such as hitting them or even shouting at them, is counterproductive. It actually makes training take longer. Goldens like fun, and they enthusiastically take to new things when they are presented in an upbeat, positive way. This requires great control over your tone of voice. Even if you are disappointed, discouraged, or suffering from a major head cold, keep your voice pleasant, encouraging, and cheerful. Goldens respond much faster to a cheerful voice.

Are all Goldens highly trainable? Probably not. Not every Golden can be a service dog or a drug detection dog. Not every Golden can be an obedience champion. Each of those occupations requires certain traits that must be in the dog from the start. But the typical Golden can learn enough to become a very good family friend and companion. Wise dog owners will work with their Goldens every day, decide which commands are essential, and insist that their dogs follow those rules. Goldens can learn to stay off the furniture, not jump on people, and walk on a leash. Somebody just has to tell them that those things are important.

SUPPLIES
FOR YOUR
GOLDEN RETRIEVER

Dog stores, catalogs, and websites are filled with glitzy stuff for the dog of your dreams. But your real dog only needs a few things to be safe and healthy—and those things don't have to be designer brands. Many dog owners are crafty recyclers and their dogs thrive.

Outfitting a 60- or 70-pound (27- or 31.5-kg) dog requires an eye for durability and a knowledge of your individual Golden. Goldens as a group are big dogs who jump in puddles or snowbanks, roll in leaves, and like to shake dead fish or squirrels. And the Golden in your household will have his own variations on this theme. Some are almost fastidious, while others live covered with mud. You'll need to invest in a working washing machine and high-quality vacuum cleaner.

BED

Every dog needs a bed, but Goldens can be frustrating when it comes to sleeping places. Many will sleep on a cool tile floor *next* to their dog beds, especially in warm weather. Others will sleep with part of their body—even their head— hanging off a dog bed. Some will sleep with their heads hidden under your bed, behind the bed skirt—and few things are more startling than to discover a "headless dog" lying on your bedroom rug. But despite your dog's best efforts to shun it, he should still have his own bed. It gives him a comfy spot to call his own.

Puppies start off sleeping in a crate. Because they chew, only minimal bedding is required. A thin fleecy blanket, available in pet stores, or even an old towel is all they need. Save the orthopedic crate pad for another year. As your dog gets older

Delay purchasing an expensive bed until your Golden is past the chewing stage.

and is allowed to spend time outside the kitchen, a simple pillow or folded blanket may serve as a dog bed in the TV room. When he is a year or year-and-a-half old, look for a durable dog bed with a cover that can be removed and washed.

During his first six months, watch how your dog sleeps when he is not in his crate. Goldens usually sprawl on their sides, but some sleep curled up. If you have a dog who sleeps stretched out, look for a rectangular bed. You will need a large size, at least 24 by 36 inches (61 by 91.5 cm), and bigger is better if you have the space, 42 or 48 inches (106.5 or 122 cm) long. Many dog owners have a smaller bed in an office or TV room and a larger one in the bedroom.

COLLAR

Because Goldens have an extra ruff of hair around their neck, fancy collars are hard to see. Choose a collar based on durability, safety, and water compatibility rather than appearance. Plain nylon collars that are about 1 inch (2.5 cm) wide are best. They fasten with a buckle or quick-release mechanism and dry readily if they get wet in rain or snow.

Choose a collar based on durability, safety, and water compatibility.

Collars come in sizes to match your dog's neck; you want a collar that measures the circumference of your dog's neck in inches (cm), plus a couple of extra inches (cm). Puppies outgrow several collars before they reach full size. Check your puppy's collar frequently to make sure that it is loose enough so that you can fit two or three fingers inside it but not so loose that he can slip it over his head.

Most pet stores welcome dogs on leashes, so if you have an older puppy or a young dog, take him to the store to be fitted for his new collar. If he is almost fully grown, start with a collar that is about 20 inches (51 cm) long. Goldens' neck sizes vary by as much as 2 or 3 inches (5 or 7.5 cm), so be ready to adjust.

Prong collars—a chain with exposed metal tines that grab a dog's neck—should never be used with Goldens. These dogs are too sensitive for such a device.

CRATE

Crates are good for dogs. It's a mantra you might repeat when you put your puppy to bed at night. He is safe in the crate, and he is also learning good habits.

Buy a large crate—at least 36 inches (91.5 cm) long. If you have a big male Golden or one from a supersize line, get the 42-inch (106.5 cm) crate. Look for an enclosure with a divider so that you can block off most of the space for the first few weeks, giving your puppy just enough room to stand up and turn around. He needs that much space to stretch, but any more space and he might be tempted to relieve himself in the back corner.

WIRE CRATES

Wire crates often come with a divider, and they have other advantages: Your dog can see out and you can see in; they have good ventilation; they fold for travel; and they are spacious and allow your pet to stand fully upright.

PLASTIC CRATES

Some owners favor molded plastic crates. They do not need to be draped with towels to provide shade or coverage, and they create an excellent den-type feeling for the dog. Plastic crates may be easier to move from room to room, and if airline approved for travel, they can protect your dog. Be sure to get one with cross ventilation.

EXERCISE PEN

An ex-pen is optional and of dubious long-term value. It may be helpful with a puppy, especially if you travel a lot. But Goldens do not thrive in ex-pens. They are too big for all but the largest, most expensive ex-pens and will spend most the time in the ex-pen looking at you, asking what's next. If you don't have a fence, it is better to put your Golden on a leash and take him for a walk.

FOOD AND WATER BOWLS

Your dog needs at least two bowls: a large one for water and a slightly smaller one for food. If you buy a matching pair, buy both in the large water size—Goldens have large mouths and drink a lot of water. (An extra bowl or two for water is good if you have a deck, patio, or fenced yard. Also, you may want a travel set if you take car trips.)

Buy porcelain or stainless steel bowls that are sturdy enough to withstand strong nudges if they are left on the floor because your dog will push against the dish, licking out the last crumb, and knock it into the wall. Also, the bowls should be dishwasher safe.

Stay away from plastic bowls. This type can develop hairline cracks that collect bacteria, and some dogs are allergic to plastic.

A waterproof mat under the bowls can stop some bowl skidding and absorb water that drips off your dog's chin.

GATE

Gates are optional but come in very handy. Dog catalogs sell a wide variety of gates that can be used at the top or bottom of a stairway, at the doorway to a room that you want to keep your dog in or out of, or on a deck. Some baby gates can even be used for dogs.

Ex-pens may be helpful with a puppy, but you won't need one for an adult Golden.

Look for a gate that is at least 3 feet (1 m) high. Some Goldens will climb a gate that has footholds and others will jump it, but a Golden who has been raised with a gate will honor its message—stay put!

GROOMING SUPPLIES

Even if you intend to pay a groomer to take regular care of your Golden, you'll still need a few grooming tools at home for daily maintenance and emergency care.

BRUSH AND COMB

Goldens should be brushed once or twice a week and anytime they pick up burrs or twigs in the woods. They also need to be thoroughly brushed after they get wet, such as after a bath or a swim.

Buy a large pin brush. Find one that fits your hand and feels comfortable. They come with wooden or plastic handles and are available in a range of different prices. A metal comb with large, widely spaced teeth is also helpful. This can get through all the layers of hair down to the skin—helpful in removing dead hair— but be careful until you learn how to use it. It can pull the hair and hurt your dog, especially in sensitive area such as the stomach and groin.

FOOTBATH

A bucket or large flat plastic pan near the door is handy, and pool supply stores sell footbaths. This will allow you to rinse your Golden's feet if he has been playing in the mud, run through freshly cut wet grass that sticks to his hair, or walked on freshly fertilized grass or salted sidewalks. Keep a towel nearby.

NAIL CLIPPERS

Goldens have large toenails that need to be clipped between once a week and every two weeks. Buy a large nail clipper designed for dogs that feels comfortable in your hand.

Some groomers use a nail grinder to wear down toenails and smooth the rough edges. Nail grinders are available in many dog catalogs, but they are noisy, and some Goldens are afraid of them.

Purchase a large nail clipper made for dogs.

SCISSORS

A Golden is supposed to be a natural-looking dog, yet you should consider two kinds of scissors: regular and thinning shears. Regular scissors are required to trim the hair on the feet and the ears and to cut out mats. Thinning shears are optional but are useful if you have a dog with a heavy coat. Professional groomers use thinning shears to reduce the hair on the chest, around the ears, and on the dog's rear. The hair lies flatter and looks sleeker.

Dog Tale

When I was learning how to cut my first dog's toenails, I nicked the quick several times. After that, she hid behind chairs when I picked up the nail clippers. Now, I have two dogs who see the nail clippers in my hand, lie down flat on the floor, and hold up their paws. But the third, the youngest, resists almost as much as my first dog!

Another kind of hair thinner is a rake-type instrument with razor-like sharpness, sold under several brand names. This can be used if you are not showing your dog. Experiment on a small spot on your dog's coat, noting carefully if the blade breaks the outercoat or if it successfully rakes out the dead undercoat.

SHAMPOO

Goldens need to be shampooed every few months in winter, more frequently in warmer, muddier weather. Sometimes just their feet need a quick bath. Buy a high-quality general dog shampoo—human shampoo has the wrong pH. Check the bottle you are buying to see if it needs to be diluted before use. Tea tree oil is a good specialty shampoo, or look for dog shampoos for sensitive skin. Choose a shampoo that rinses out quickly and completely.

TOWELS

An old beach towel is the best towel to use to dry a Golden. It may take two or three towels to do the job, especially if you have a heavily coated dog.

New microfiber towels, which absorb more water, are available in dog sizes and may appeal to you. But if you don't want to buy a special towel for your dog, use old towels of any size. Just have two or three on hand for every bath.

A pile of old towels is a valuable asset with a Golden. Keep a couple in the car and by every door to wipe feet or a rainy coat before he comes back in the house. Wash doggy towels in hot water, with detergent and bleach.

IDENTIFICATION

Every dog should carry identification. ID will help him find his way home should he ever become lost.

TAGS

A collar tag is the simplest, easiest, and most helpful ID option if your dog ever gets distracted by a squirrel and takes off. Buy a tag that either hangs from an S hook on his collar (available at hardware stores and much sturdier than the loops that come with tags) or a tag that attaches to the collar itself with rivets or short nails. ID tags are sold at major pet stores and online, and come in a wide range of prices.

Put your dog's name on the tag, as well as two phone numbers. Use at least one cell number so that the finder of your dog can call you even if you lose your pet at a highway rest stop far from home. If you spend much time at a second home, make a second set of tags with that information on them. If you spend a lot of time online, put your e-mail address on the tag.

MICROCHIPS

Many breeders microchip their puppies. A microchip is a tiny piece of technology the size of a grain of rice that contains identification information and is injected into the puppy just under his skin. Animal shelters have scanners that can read the chip in case your dog is turned in. Your breeder will give you the details if she has put a chip in your puppy.

Vets have scanners, too, so you should have your new dog—puppy or rescue— scanned for a chip. The vet should scan the chip occasionally over the years to make sure that it is still readable.

LEASH

A leash is your dog's ticket to adventure. A good walking leash is about 6 feet (2 m) long and about 1 inch (2.5 cm) wide. Pick a leash that feels good in your hands. What makes a good leash good is up to you: Some people like the feel of leather; others like the inexpensiveness and washability of nylon. Some prefer flat nylon leashes and others like nylon that has been rolled into a round shape. You may want a leash that matches your dog's collar, or you may decide to buy several leashes and use them for different occasions—leather for the daily walk, nylon for a spare leash in the car, different colors for each dog, etc.

To improve your grip on the leash, either tie some knots into it or buy a knotted leather leash.

Avoid chain leashes. They'll hurt your hands, can twist around the dog's muzzle or leg, and may cut into his skin. Also, avoid skinny flimsy leashes that might snap if your dog takes off suddenly.

Goldens can be the perfect dog for a retractable leash, a long leash that snaps back into a plastic housing. It allows your dog to rove ahead of you, sniffing

Pick a leash that feels good in your hands.

and getting twice as much exercise as you do. A suitable retractable leash for a Golden is one designed for dogs heavier than 50 pounds (22.5 kg). The best have wide straps or bands for the entire 16 or 20 feet (5 or 6 m) of length. They are better for use late at night or early in the morning, in areas with few people about. They are not appropriate for busy city sidewalks, crowded beaches, therapy dog work, or visits to classrooms. Dogs on retractable leashes will not learn to heel or to not pull. It is best to teach your dog those behaviors on a standard 6-foot (2-m) leash and switch to the retractable leash for pleasure walking. Retractable leashes should be viewed as a reward or a sort of "mini-vacation" for your dog.

TOYS

Modern dogs who spend their time in a house or fenced yard absolutely must have toys.

CHEW TOYS

Chew toys are the first need, especially for young dogs. Large, hard, durable bones made of rubber or plastic and sold by reputable companies are a must. Knotted ropes also appeal to some Goldens. All chew toys wear down after a while and should be checked regularly to see if broken sections could pose a choking hazard to your dog.

Goldens like to carry things in their mouths, and they should be provided with soft fleecy toys; these can be as simple as knotted strips or be shaped like stuffed animals. (They *do* have imaginations and like to pretend some toys are dead ducks.) Many Goldens are happy to carry around knotted ropes, shaking them occasionally to make sure they're "dead." Squeakers are optional; some Goldens will chew out the squeaker to see what is making the noise, and so play with squeaker toys should always be supervised.

FLOATING TOYS

If you can find a safe lake or pond for swimming, a floating toy is a good buy. Bumpers—long skinny plastic toys that resemble the bumpers boaters use to protect their boats from scraping against docks—are perfect. Many come in bright orange, a color that's easy to spot in the water.

STUFFABLE TOYS

Stuffable rubber toys are frequently touted as a good dog toy, but they are too simple for some Goldens. A hunk of smelly rubber that is impossible to shake just isn't interesting to your Golden. But if you buy him a rubber toy covered in a durable nylon fabric with streaming tails of fabric, your Golden may change his mind. The fabric has a better mouth feel, and the tails hang out of his mouth so that he can shake it. It can also be used as a fetch toy.

TENNIS BALLS

Tennis balls should also be used only with supervision. Your Golden may start chewing on one, but it was not designed with that in mind. Real tennis balls that

Most Goldens will love a floating toy that can be used in water.

have been used and aged in a bag in the basement seem to last longer than fresh ones out of the can or even those designed for dogs.

TRAVEL EQUIPMENT

Most Goldens love a car trip. If you take your dog in the car, bring a leash, towel or blanket for him to sit on, water, and a bowl.

Goldens should never ride in the front seat because of the potential danger from the passenger air bag. If you step on the brake suddenly, he could hit the windshield.

In the backseat, Goldens can be restrained with dog harnesses that attach to seat belts. In a van or minivan, your Golden can travel in his crate. Special wire crates are available that fit side by side in the back of a minivan for people with multiple dogs. Some Golden owners who often travel by car build platforms under the crates to lift them so that their dogs can see out the window. In SUVs or minivans, the large back area can become your dog's own traveling home away from home, with a pressure gate fitted to prevent him from moving forward. He'll still need to be restrained when the vehicle is moving, but when you're parked for a rest stop, he can be allowed to get up and move around inside his space. Remember, though, that you must never leave any dog unattended in a parked vehicle.

FEEDING YOUR GOLDEN RETRIEVER

When it comes to choosing foods for your Golden, you may wish for a choreographer to help you make all the right moves. But the truth is, no one can tell you what to feed your dog. Each dog, each budget, and each household adds just enough uniqueness to the mix that the decision has to be uniquely yours. Dog diets have as many twists as there are owners, and the only thing they have in common is that somebody made a choice. Read labels, read recipes, think about what you can do every day, compare diets and brands, and make a choice based on what is best for you and your dog.

NUTRIENTS

Your Golden grows, fights off disease, and produces the energy he needs to chase tennis balls solely on the fuel you give him. Dogs eat many kinds of food—meat, fish, fruits, vegetables, and grains such as oats and rice. Your job is to balance those foods so that he gets the essential elements he needs to grow, stay healthy, and chase squirrels.

The gold standard in designing a balanced diet comes from the Association of American Feed Control Officials (AAFCO), a nonprofit national organization. Commercial dog foods that want to label themselves "complete and balanced" must meet all of the AAFCO's standards or pass a feeding trial. Once they have done so, their packages can carry the AAFCO seal. Although not regulated in the same way, a home-cooked diet should be just as balanced and meet the AAFCO standard as well. An all-meat diet, for example, is not enough.

The AAFCO specifies both minimum and maximum amounts for some nutrients, such as minerals and vitamins. It dictates minimums for others, such as protein. Learning to read a label on commercial foods or calculate the content of a homemade stew is an important skill for dog owners. But you already know the two biggest factors in a healthy diet for dogs because they are the same as they are for people: balance and portion control.

CARBOHYDRATES

Carbohydrates turn into energy inside your dog. They power that beautiful running gait over snowy trails. Most commercial dog food has more carbohydrates than anything else—much more than a dog in the wild would eat—because they are cheaper, and some, like rice and corn, are more easily digested than some meat by-products, like feathers and bones. Those that aren't digested provide the fiber that improves colon health and stool firmness.

Carbohydrates, usually grains such as wheat, oats, corn, rice, and barley, make commercial kibble possible. They provide the structure that holds it together. But

The two biggest factors in a healthy diet for dogs are balance and portion control.

the danger is that many dogs get more carbohydrates than they need, resulting in obesity. Dogs who run in agility or field trials burn more carbohydrates than dogs who are couch potatoes. In the same way, dogs who swim every day need more carbs than those who don't. The best dog owners adjust their dog's diet to his activity level.

FATS

Fats are a very important part of a dog's diet. They help that stunning Golden coat flow in the wind and shine in the sun. Fats carry fat-soluble vitamins and fatty acids, such as omega-3 and omega-6, that are crucial to your dog's health. Fats also add energy, make food taste good, and contribute to muscle tone and skin and coat health. A no-fat or even a diet that's too low in fat could end up causing trouble in many ways. But this nutrient category includes many different types of fats. Some fats are better for your dog than others, and a variety is best. Different kinds of fats contain different vitamins and acids. Fish oil has more of the good fat that dogs need than does beef fat. But all fat has to be part of a balanced diet—a small part of it. Dogs who eat a lot of fat all at once—such as cleaning up after a Thanksgiving turkey—can develop pancreatitis, an illness of the pancreas. And dogs who eat too much fat every day end up obese. It's a balancing act.

MINERALS

Twelve minerals make the AAFCO list of required nutrients for dogs: calcium, chloride, copper, iodine, iron, phosphorous, potassium, sodium, magnesium, manganese, selenium, and zinc. Commercial dog foods that have the AAFCO seal on the package include these minerals, so you don't have to give them a second thought. If you serve a homemade diet, you'll have to add a multivitamin supplement with minerals, as advised by your vet.

Your Golden needs minerals for good bone and cartilage health, as well as muscle, nerve, and even hormonal functions. But adding one or two minerals won't work. Minerals work in conjunction with each other and with vitamins. It's that balance thing again!

Fats in your Golden's diet contribute to his skin and coat health.

PROTEINS

A minimum of 18 percent of an adult dog's food should be protein according to the AAFCO's "dry matter" standard. Those proteins should contain ten amino acids your dog needs, and that are found in different meats and plants . . . so a steady diet of steak just won't be enough. Your dog requires a balanced variety of protein found in poultry, fish, beef, and even plants such as soybeans, corn, and wheat. The better the poultry, fish, or beef, the better the quality of protein your dog gets. Generally, commercial kibble has more than one protein unless it is marked "one protein." A homemade diet should include several proteins.

VITAMINS

Eleven vitamins are on the AAFCO list as part of a balanced canine diet. They are as familiar as vitamins A, D, and E and as complicated as eight types of B (B1, B2, B3, B5, B6, B12, choline, and folic acid). What is not required is Vitamin C because dogs make their own. Vitamin C is sometimes used as a supplement for specific situations but does not have to be added to the ordinary dog's daily diet.

The eleven required vitamins are essential for a dog's metabolism to work properly. Some are fat soluble and some are water soluble. The fat-soluble vitamins—A, D, and E—are stored in the body, but the water soluble ones—the B complex—are not. The two types have opposite dangers: Too much of the fat-soluble vitamins can lead to an overdose, and too little of the water-soluble ones can lead to a deficit.

Commercial dog food carrying the AAFCO seal includes vitamins. Supplementing a commercial diet needs to be done thoughtfully or not at all because overloading your dog with one vitamin can be just as dangerous as depriving him. Home-cooked diets should include an added multivitamin; check with your vet to see which type she recommends.

WATER

Ordinary fresh water is one of the most important things you can give your Golden. He needs a large, clean dish full of water available day and night. Water prevents dehydration and helps cool dogs who are panting after exercise or exposure to heat. It also aids in digestion; dogs who eat dry kibble will drink more water.

Avoid placing the dish where things can fall in the water. Rinse the bowl twice a day and scrub it with soap often. Goldens drink a lot of water, dripping extra off their chins, so place the bowl on a large mat.

If you can drink the tap water, so can your dog, but if you drink bottled or filtered water for safety reasons, he should too.

Your Golden needs a large, clean dish full of water available day and night.

COMMERCIAL FOODS

Shelves loaded with commercial dog food today include many good choices for Goldens. Breeders who try to convince you that only one brand is good for a dog are mistaken. Your Golden will thrive on many brands of commercial food, but the shelves also contain some very poor choices. Your breeder will probably try to help you avoid a bad choice by steering you to one she trusts.

Dog Tale

Our dogs love raw carrots. They come from anywhere in the house as soon as they hear the sound of the knife chopping carrots. They sit and wait for me to toss carrots at them to catch.

Many manufacturers of commercial foods test the formula they use, tweaking it as the years go by to improve it. Those are the foods you are looking for. Commercial dog food comes in dry kibble, semi-moist, and canned versions. Kibble and canned are the best choices for Goldens, and either is better than a steady diet of table scraps. Scraps may not include all the nutrients a dog needs, and they may contain some things that are dangerous to him, such as onions, grapes, and small cooked bones that may splinter in his digestive tract.

DRY FOOD

Dry food, or kibble, is a very popular choice for Goldens. It is economical, stores well, travels well, and is easy to serve. Golden owners are the ones you see buying 40-pound (18-kg) bags at the pet food store, sometimes two at a time. However, purchase only what your pet can consume in a few months. Dry food does go stale, and it loses some of its nutrients over time. Store the food in the bag it comes in, inside a plastic bin with a tight seal. This will keep your dog from helping himself, and the food will remain as fresh as possible.

Dry food comes in a large-breed formula that is good for Goldens; in addition to a combination of ingredients designed for larger dogs, the large-breed formulas have larger pieces of kibble that make it harder for Goldens to inhale food up their noses. (Enthusiastic Goldens eat so fast that they have been known to do this.)

As a practical matter, always measure dry food with a measuring cup. Start with slightly less than the package recommends, and add or subtract with an eye to your dog and how many treats you offer throughout the day. If he starts to gain more weight than he should, cut back on treats first but also on kibble. All dogs don't need the full portion that the manufacturer recommends. A Golden on a premium dog food may need as little as 2 $\frac{1}{2}$ cups a day. A large Golden in performance sports such as agility may need 4 cups a day.

How to Choose a Dry Food

Choose a dry food by comparing the first five ingredients on the package. An animal protein such as chicken or chicken meal should be both the first ingredient and should appear one more time in the first five. Even more important is to avoid packages that have corn or rice three times in the first five ingredients (such as corn, cornmeal, and corn gluten meal) because the grain can add up to more than the animal protein. Corn can be harder to digest, and some dogs—but not all—are allergic to it. Corn is a controversial ingredient, scorned by some dog owners but well tolerated by enough dogs that it appears in many dry foods. Make a decision about corn based on your own dog's performance, not on what you read on the Internet. Many Goldens do well with some corn in a dry food, while others do not. In any case, some whole grains are desirable. Vegetables are good. Avoid sugar anywhere in the ingredients.

Supplementing kibble with whole foods is a good way to boost the fresh nutrition you offer your dog and make sure that he gets some unprocessed food. Several times a week, feed him cooked beef, chicken, or fish after cutting off the fat. Add fresh bananas, apple slices, blueberries, chunks of cooked sweet potato, carrots, peas, or green beans—raw or cooked but without sauces or salt. Some of these can be offered as treats or training rewards. Others can be mixed into the dry food. Reduce the amount of kibble up to 1/4 cup on a night when you have baked chicken to give your dog.

Rhonda Hovan, Golden breeder and Golden Retriever Club of America (GRCA) health and nutrition expert, says that cruciferous vegetables, such as broccoli, should be a part of a Golden's diet. "In order for the dog to get the benefit of the broccoli, the cell walls have to be broken down. It should be raw but chopped very finely or pureed. Mix it in with the dry food," she says.

SEMI-MOIST FOOD

Some dog foods are designed for the people who buy them rather than for the dog who eats them. Semi-moist foods fall into that category. These foods

PUPPY POINTER

Obese puppies are in double trouble—now, when they should be running and learning things that active puppies need to know, and later, when their joints just give out after a lifetime of carrying extra weight.

come in a pouch because they have more moisture than dry food. They are the least desirable of the commercial foods from many standpoints because they frequently contain more sugar, salt, chemicals, and preservatives than do dry or canned foods. Save them for a rare, special treat.

How to Choose a Semi-Moist Food
Semi-moist foods used as treats should be something your dog really wants. Choose a treat based on the reaction you get from your dog when you are training the *come* command. (See Chapter 7.) Also, choose a treat that can be broken into small parts, like bacon strip treats.

CANNED FOOD
Canned dog foods can be a nutritious choice for your Golden every day or as an occasional treat or supplement if they contain a high-quality protein.

Dog food labels are highly regulated by federal and state governments, and the ingredients must be listed in order by weight. The U.S. Food and Drug Administration (FDA) has a 95 percent rule for canned dog foods. If a can says just "beef," it must be 95 percent beef, not counting water or condiments. If the can has less than 95 percent, it must be labeled with descriptive words such as "beef dinner" or "platter." Read the label carefully. Both good and bad canned foods sit on the same shelves.

Canned dog foods can be a nutritious choice for your Golden.

The good cans have high-quality animal proteins and fewer preservatives than dry food. Even the hard-to-please *Whole Dog Journal*, a respected publication that ranks dog foods annually, has come out in favor of canned food as a healthy option for dogs for those two reasons—better quality proteins and less preservatives. Canned foods have always been the number-one choice for picky eaters or dogs who need more liquid in their diet. Canned food now comes in organic and whole grain varieties, as well as in varieties that include fish, chunks of beef or chicken, sweet potatoes, and carrots.

How to Choose a Canned Food

Read the label as carefully as you would a dry food label. Concentrate on the first five ingredients, looking for whole meats or fish, whole grains or vegetables, and no sugar. Some canned foods have vitamins and minerals. Know what you are giving your dog so that you can complete the mix he needs.

NONCOMMERCIAL FOODS

For centuries, dogs ate noncommercial foods. Nobody bought packaged dog food. Our pets ate what we ate as we evolved together. They filled in gaps in their diet with what they caught in the field, pulled off a bush, or found in the garbage. So, without a doubt your dog can *exist* on a noncommercial or homemade diet—but it takes skill on your part to know what he needs and the time to provide it so that he will *thrive*.

If you have the interest and the time, you can cook for your dog, throw in some vitamin and mineral supplements, and watch him shine. Or you could feed him a raw diet that attempts to duplicate what dogs ate in the wild. This also takes time and research.

Noncommercial diets must be balanced and contain all the essential nutrients your dog needs: carbohydrates, fats, minerals, proteins, and vitamins. They are a desirable option if the commercial dog foods you have tried just aren't working for your dog.

Goldens are voracious eaters, and most will scarf down whatever you feed them. But they are also known as a breed with allergies, and some of those allergies are to foods. If your dog is not thriving on the commercial food you are feeding, he might be allergic to the corn, wheat, beef, or something else that's in it. Some dogs with allergy symptoms do better on home-cooked or raw diets.

HOME-COOKED DIET

A home-cooked diet requires research, recipes, fresh ingredients, and cooking for your dog. It is not simply a matter of offering your Golden the leftovers from your meals.

BE AWARE!

Plain or vanilla yogurt can slow an unsettled stomach and settle digestive upsets caused by eating the wrong things in the yard. Half a cup works well—a little less or a little more depending on what kind of week your Golden has had.

Start by researching canine menus that include all of the nutrients your dog needs. Look for recipes for stews, baked dinners, or sautéed fish and vegetables. A well-rounded home-cooked diet includes variety—chicken, beef, turkey, and fish (unless your dog is allergic to one of those). It requires no salt or sugar, but it does need some fat or oil.

Make a shopping list of the ingredients you'll need. Include a canine multivitamin with minerals (after consulting with your vet). To save time in the long run, cook several meals at once and freeze some portions for later in the week.

Obviously, a home-cooked diet for a dog as big as a Golden will require calorie calculations to make sure that he gets enough but not too much. Consult a veterinarian for help in getting started. For a fee, some veterinary schools will provide nutritional analysis of the diet you have put together. Experts in canine nutrition have written books on cooking for your dog that you should consult, such as *The Healthy Dog Cookbook*.

The satisfaction in providing a well-constructed home-cooked meal is genuine and deep, and watching a previously listless dog thrive is exciting. Those two goals are enough to make many Golden owners happy cooks. But cooking for dogs is not for everyone. Dogs have to eat twice a day, every day, and Goldens eat a big dish of food at every meal. If you are not an experienced cook or shopper, try other options before you attempt cooking 14 meals a week for your dog.

One solution many dog owners have adopted is a combination of dry food and home cooked. The dog gets 14 meals a week of a premium kibble, and that guarantees the vitamins and minerals and overall nutritional balance. He also gets four or five supplemental feedings a week of home-cooked chicken, beef, fish, and vegetables and fruits, which add fresh unprocessed food to his diet. (The amount of kibble you feed per day should vary depending on the amount of fresh food you're giving your Golden.)

RAW DIET

The raw diet mimics what the wolf ate in the wild, since dogs are descended from wolves. It includes raw meat, uncooked bones, raw eggs, and fruits and vegetables. Raw diets can now be bought, in frozen form, at some pet food stores.

This diet has been controversial from the time it first became popular. Those who feed it say that their dogs flourish. One raw diet company says that its customers notice shiny, healthy skin and coats in their dogs and that the dogs fed this raw diet have cleaner teeth, better-smelling breath, smaller stools, fewer allergy symptoms, and more energy.

Feeding a raw diet requires the ability to purchase fresh raw meat regularly or store frozen raw food safely. It also requires the understanding of how to supplement the raw diet so that the dog has complete nutrition. Raw diet advocates are unequivocal in their enthusiasm for raw meat. But others, including vets, caution that it is very difficult to get the nutritional balance right in a raw diet. Also, raw foods have to be handled carefully and cleaned up after religiously

A raw diet requires a lot of research on your part.

to prevent human exposure to *Salmonella* and *E. coli* that may be present. Dogs who eat a raw diet may carry bacteria that can be harmful to small children or immune-compromised people.

Golden breeder and nutrition expert Rhonda Hovan is skeptical of the claims raw food advocates make. "In feeding a dog, there are huge misconceptions all over the Internet, people who take diet to an extreme," she says. "There is a lot of very good science to support the benefits of diets made by major companies that are doing the research. I would be much more suspect of small companies, these boutique companies. They don't have as much data and science behind

Most Goldens love to eat—they will eat whatever and however often you feed them.

what they do. And raw diets—zero science. None whatsoever supports a raw diet. All the claims are just somebody talking."

Hovan says that published studies looked at contamination of raw food and how the dogs who eat them shed more *Salmonella* and *E. coli* in their feces than did dogs who eat cooked foods. After analyzing those studies, the Delta Society, in 2010, banned the raw diet for dogs in their service dog program. They did it to protect babies and immune-compromised people in the families their dogs serve.

WHEN TO FEED

Goldens love to eat, and it is fun to feed them. But restrain your joy to twice a day.

Feed your Golden once in the morning and once in the evening, as close to 12 hours apart as you can. Divide the food for the day in half and feed half at each meal. (Goldens are always looking for more food, and if you feed them everything at breakfast you will have nothing left to give them at dinner.) Smaller meals are better for your dog. Goldens tend to gulp their food and so could develop bloat, a serious and sometimes fatal condition in which the stomach twists over.

Whatever you do, do not attempt to keep the food dish full and allow your Golden to free feed whenever he wants. Only a few Goldens can restrain themselves from scarfing up the whole thing at once, and in fact most will eat

GOLDEN RETRIEVER

whatever and however often you feed them. They will end up weighing 100 pounds (45.5 kg) before they are two years old!

OBESITY

Obesity has been called the most common nutritional disorder in dogs. Dogs get fat just the way people do—too many calories going in and not enough going out. Then those excess calories turn to fat.

Keeping your dog trim requires a double-edged plan: feeding him just as much food as he needs and exercising him more. This is especially important because obesity is thought to be a contributing factor in many serious Golden health conditions, including cancer, orthopedic problems, and even early death. Your Golden will always want more to eat, so it is up to you to measure his food and stick to a plan, even when he is a puppy. Pudgy puppies may not be as healthy as smaller, leaner ones.

Rhonda Hovan has developed a slow-growth plan for Golden puppies up to four months old that can be retrieved from the Golden Retriever Club of America's website (www.grca.o2rg). Slowing the growth of young puppies can help their bones and joints develop better. Obesity is hard on joints, especially developing ones. Hovan recommends weighing puppies, cutting training treats down to the smallest possible bit, feeding large-breed puppy food, and beginning serious exercise starting at eight weeks of age. At eight weeks, she suggests that a Golden puppy should weigh only 9.5 pounds (4.5 kg), at 16 weeks only 22 to 23 pounds (10 to 10.5 kg), and at 20 weeks, 30 pounds (13.5 kg) or less. An eight-week-old puppy can walk 1/2 mile (1.5 km), she says, four or five times a week, gradually increasing this distance until he can walk 3 miles (5 km) at 18 weeks. This is a walk, not a jog or a run, she says, and it is best done on a grassy path in a park. Of course, if you are starting with an 18-week-old puppy, begin at 1/2 mile (1.5 km) and build up gradually, she recommends.

"You'll have a dog so beautifully leash trained, you won't even have to think about leash training," she says. "What they really need is exercise to keep the muscles strong to support the joints. The dogs become so much more well mannered in the house when they are getting enough exercise. Exercise is really important—even if playing in the yard is [all that] you can do [on occasion], then do it."

GROOMING YOUR GOLDEN RETRIEVER

Newcomers to Golden Retrievers, watching that glorious golden coat ripple in the sun, often say "That coat must take a lot of work." The good news is that it's not as much work as you'd think—unless you are showing your dog in conformation. "It's not a terrible amount of work for a pet," Amy Booth, professional dog handler says. "But it's a lot of work for a dog show." The Golden coat was designed for hunting in rough countryside and for retrieving in duck ponds. After a good shake, water, mud, and dirty snow fly in every direction—off the dog. When the coat completely dries, mud can be easily brushed off. And even better, the outercoat is tangle-resistant. Only the white undercoat mats and needs to be brushed regularly.

Golden owners know that a little attention now means a beautiful sight tomorrow—that gorgeous coat contrasting with the green grass or the white snow, flowing in the wind.

WHY GROOMING IS IMPORTANT

"Grooming" is a catchall word that includes everything it takes to keep your Golden's body in top shape, including his coat, teeth, ears, eyes, and nails. As part of a regular grooming routine, experienced owners check for things that may need to be seen by a vet: a rash, a hot spot, a lump, an infected wound, inflamed ears, or even just a bald spot. All of these things can be indicators of much more serious issues, and spotting them early will help your Golden heal faster.

But grooming has another plus that is not physical. It is time for you and your Golden to bond, and he'll get the one-on-one attention he craves. You can make him feel special, reinforce some commands such as stay, and focus on what makes him happy. Grooming is a time when you can learn things about each other that you can build on in every activity.

GROOMING SUPPLIES

What you use to keep your Golden in good shape depends on your preferences. Grooming tools are a highly personal choice. Pet stores and catalogs sell a dizzying variety of tools and gadgets that will either help you or end up cluttering your dog shelf.

Tool prices range from professional and expensive to so cheap that they are useless. For a big dog with a full coat like the Golden, buy at least the medium-priced options. The teeth on inexpensive combs will bend under the weight of a Golden coat, inexpensive shampoo can dry his coat and skin, and inexpensive pin brushes will not stand up to the task.

At least in the beginning, try to buy tools at stores or dog shows so that you can

You can use an old bath towel or beach towel to dry your Golden.

pick them up and feel them in your hand. A nail clipper that doesn't feel comfortable in your hand is a nail clipper that will get used less and less frequently.

Dog owners who intend to have their dog professionally bathed and groomed will need only a few tools for emergencies: shampoo for late night rolls in smelly stuff, towels, a pin brush, and toothpaste and toothbrush. For those who do most of the grooming themselves, the list is longer.

BLADED RAKE

A bladed rake is an optional piece of equipment, but it can remove dead hair quickly if used carefully and only occasionally.

COMB

A large-toothed comb, sometimes called a Greyhound comb, will reach all the way through the coat to the skin, thoroughly removing tangles and dead hair. But this means that it must be used gently—especially on the belly. Avoid scraping the skin or roughly pulling on tangles.

CONDITIONER

Goldens with dry skin may benefit from a dog conditioner. (Don't use human hair products because they don't contain the correct pH balance for your dog.) Conditioners are optional for dogs not going into a show ring.

GROOMING TABLE

A full-sized table is an optional piece of equipment that will allow you to work on your dog without sitting on the floor or bending over.

HAIR DRYER

This piece of equipment is also optional. If you choose to invest in a hair dryer, purchase one that has cool or warm settings. Never use the hot setting on your dog, or you could burn him.

NAIL CLIPPERS

Look for medium to large guillotine-type or scissors-type dog nail clippers that fit your hand. Human clippers just aren't effective against the Golden's thick, curved nails. The guillotine type has a blade on only one side and can leave a sharp edge on your dog's nail. The scissors type looks more like pruning shears; it has blades on both sides, like scissors do, and it also leaves a sharp edge on the nail. Electric nail sanders leave smooth edges, but they make a noise that some dogs may not tolerate, especially older dogs. Show dog groomers prefer them.

PUPPY POINTER

Groom your puppy right from the beginning so that he learns it is part of everyday life. Keep sessions short and fun. Use only your pin brush, and brush lightly. Say "Stand" and offer your puppy lots of treats for complying.

PIN BRUSH

The basic go-to grooming tool, a pin brush helps sort out the coat, brush out debris, and head off mats. Its flexible pins are attached to a rubber base and are tapered but not pointed or sharp. They may not reach all the way to the skin in some parts of the coat on some dogs, but this is the tool you should reach for after your Golden has rolled in a pile of leaves or even a dry dusty spot. Buy a large-headed brush with a handle that fits your hand.

SCISSORS

Sharp scissors that are used only on dog hair are essential to trim the feet and ears and cut out mats. These can be dog scissors, barber scissors, or high-quality household scissors. Some people like full-sized scissors, but many people use a smaller size for the feet and ears. If you have a full-coated dog, thinning scissors are useful on the ruff around his neck, the hairs in his ears, and the hair on his rear end.

SHAMPOO

Use only canine shampoo because, like conditioner, it has the proper pH for dogs. Human shampoo is slightly too acidic for dogs. Buy a small bottle of a good-quality dog shampoo and try it out. Look for shampoos that say "moisturizing" or "easy to rinse." Once you find a shampoo that you like and that agrees with your dog, buy a large bottle.

TOOTHPASTE AND TOOTHBRUSH
Buy canine toothpaste—not human toothpaste—because it foams less and can be swallowed. For a toothbrush, use a soft human toothbrush, a rubber thimble designed by canine toothpaste makers, or even a piece of gauze.

TOWELS
You can buy microfiber towels with your dog's name embroidered on them, or you can use old bath towels. Old beach towels are even better. You'll be surprised how many towels Goldens go through: at least two for a bath, one after every trip out to a muddy yard, one after a long walk on a rainy night (even after the rain has stopped), one on the seat of the car for a trip to the dog park, etc. Soon, a pile of clean old towels will give you a sense of security.

COAT AND SKIN CARE
A clean, just-brushed coat looks spectacular, smells good, feels great to the touch, and sheds less. What's not to like about that?

Invest in a grooming table to help with brushing.

BRUSHING

A Golden's hair needs to be brushed often. Some people brush their dogs every day, saying that it reduces doggy odor and stray hairs on the floor. But the typical Golden owner brushes her dog less often, once or twice a week. Brushing cleans out tiny pieces of grass and leaves that accumulate in a dog's coat, pulls out some dead hairs, and reduces matting. It also helps distribute skin oils and makes the hair look a little shinier.

How to Brush

1. Start with a dry dog standing in front of you, a pin brush in your hand and some treats in your pocket. On a nice day, brush your dog outside to keep flyaway hairs out of your house.
2. Hold your dog by the collar or put him on a grooming table and tether him to the table's arm. Talk to him matter-of-factly, saying "It's time to brush Ben. Ben is going to be very pretty."
3. Start brushing. If you are brushing out a specific concentration of dried mud, begin there. Otherwise, start on your dog's shoulders because they are less sensitive. Brush down the front legs and around the front to the ruff. Finish the neck, and work your way down the dog's back to his rear end. Brush the legs, tail, and the feathers on his back end.
4. Occasionally, use a wide-toothed Greyhound comb or bladed rake to get all the way down to your dog's skin and remove dead hair. Use both of these tools gently, avoiding the face and genital areas. They work best on the heavy-coated parts of the dog: the back, sides, ruff, and rear. They do not need to be used every time you brush him.
5. Ask your dog to lie down. Lift up one leg at a time and carefully brush under all four legs, watching for mats that have to be cut out in the armpits. Gently brush the stomach.

Mats form when dead hair drops off the dog and gets tangled in other hairs, and the thick Golden undercoat is the perfect environment for them. All Goldens get them, in fact. Brush or cut them out when they are still small because large mats pull on a dog's skin and are painful. Cutting out a large mat can leave an unsightly gap in your Golden's coat or tail. Cut out mats before they get big and no one will notice.

BATHING

After you have brushed your dog, you are ready to bathe him. Goldens only need a bath when they get dirty or every couple of months. In the winter, he might

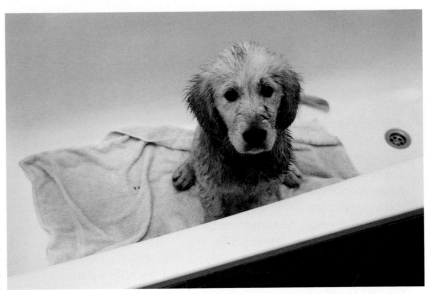

You must rinse your dog thoroughly—any shampoo left on him will cause itching.

need a bath every three months, while in the summer it may be every month.

How do you know when your dog needs a bath? He'll get a doggy odor, his coat will be flat, not fluffy, and it won't feel as soft. Aside from appearance, bathing is also important to your dog's health. It washes away any fleas, allergens, and dead hair that causes mats. It also keeps his genital area clean, reducing the chances of infection.

Before bathing your Golden, assemble two or three towels, shampoo, and get your dog into the bathroom. You can use a regular bathtub, but an enclosed stall shower works better because dogs like to shake when they get wet. (Some people buy special dog tubs that are elevated so that they don't have to bend over.) It is important to have a spray hose to wet and rinse your dog. On warm days, an outside bath with the garden hose is okay, but the wash water should not be ice cold.

1. Get in the shower with your dog—and be prepared to get wet! Test the water to make sure that it is lukewarm. Wet the dog's front end thoroughly, a process that can take several minutes because Golden coats resist water. Run your fingers through the hair under a stream of water until it penetrates to the skin.

2. Hold your dog to stop him from shaking and pour a dollop of shampoo on each shoulder. Rub the shampoo in and down both legs. Wash his front half,

adding shampoo and water as needed. Avoid getting shampoo into his eyes or ears. His face may not need any shampoo at all; the water will be enough.

3. Next, wet the back half of your dog slowly and carefully until he is soaked to the skin. Repeat the shampooing process—and don't forget the tail.

4. Rinse your dog from the front to the back. This is the hardest part. It takes many minutes to rinse all the soap out of a Golden coat. Run your fingers through his coat while you spray it with water. By now, you and your dog are probably looking forward to the end of this. But don't quit early! In fact, when you have rinsed your entire dog, go back and do it again. Shampoo left on the skin will cause him to itch.

5. Squeegee your dog with your hands. Press down on his shoulders and all the way down his legs, picking up his feet and gently squeezing the water out. Repeat with the back legs.

6. Let him shake—this is why a stall shower is great. Then grab a towel and carefully dry his head, using a damp end of the towel to wipe out his ears. Use the towel on his body, rubbing only as much as needed to avoid tangling the hair. Squeeze his body gently with the towel. (This is a command you can teach him. When he shakes, clap and say "Shake it! Good dog!" Eventually he'll learn what "shake it" means and that it makes you happy when he shakes. Meanwhile, if you rub his head with a towel and stop, he will probably shake anyway.) Then get out of the shower, get a dry towel and start drying him again.

7. Blow-dry the coat if desired, using cool or lukewarm air.

8. Brush or comb the coat before it is completely dry to remove dead hair before it mats, especially at the rear end. Wet hair that mats as it dries must be cut out.

9. Brush again the next day to finish the process.

You may need to give your Golden a footbath more frequently than a full bath. In fact, in mud season, Goldens may need a footbath two or three times a day. Buy a large plastic bin—pool supply stores sometimes have footbath trays 3 or 4 inches (7.5 or 10 cm) deep. Yard supply stores might also have large enough bins. It should be big enough for at least 2 inches (5 cm) of water and two dog feet but not so deep that it frightens your dog or requires you to lift him up and in. The idea is to wash mud off the foot, footpads, and nails without getting the whole leg or belly wet. On exceptionally muddy days, add a little diluted shampoo to the water.

DENTAL CARE

A healthy Golden does not have bad breath. He has 42 large teeth that fit nicely in a large mouth. But all creatures with teeth have to worry about plaque—an accumulation of food and bacteria along the gum line that can lead to gingivitis and periodontal disease, and eventually even heart disease as the infection moves through the blood. The plaque has to be removed occasionally, or it will turn into tartar. Chewing hard things every day will help—hard biscuits or dental treats, toys designed as plaque removers, and some raw bones. The Veterinary Oral Health Council (VOHC) tests and allows its seal to be used on products that reduce plaque and tartar, but nothing can beat brushing the teeth. A good dental hygiene program includes brushing your dog's teeth every day or at least three

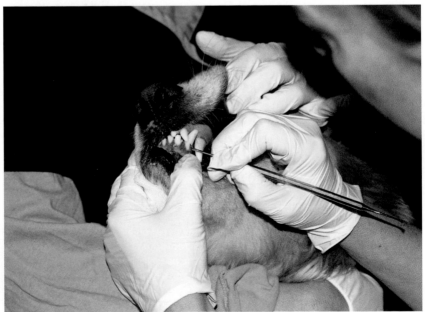

If your Golden has too much tartar buildup on his teeth, he'll need a veterinarian to scrape them.

times a week. But even brushing your dog's teeth once a week is better than never doing so.

HOW TO BRUSH THE TEETH

1. Buy dog toothpaste because it is designed to be swallowed, as well as a soft toothbrush, a rubber dog toothbrush thimble, or a piece of gauze or thin washcloth.
2. Hold your dog's muzzle in one hand and run your finger over his teeth. Then run your finger with toothpaste over his teeth. When he is used to this, brush his front teeth, top and bottom, with the other.
3. Add more toothpaste and brush the teeth on one side and then the other. Only brush the outside of the teeth because that's where most plaque builds up. (Some vets think that the tongue helps remove plaque on the inside teeth.) Go slowly. If your dog is older and not used to having his teeth brushed, try brushing one section today and another tomorrow.
4. Always praise him and offer him a treat when you are done.
   Your vet should look at your Golden's teeth at every checkup.

EAR CARE

Golden ears are easy to take care of. The most important thing is to keep them dry. Check them occasionally to be sure that they are still pale pink and pretty inside. Goldens with allergies sometimes get ear infections that turn their ears angry red, and those who swim a lot sometimes get hot spots near their ears.

HOW TO CARE FOR THE EARS

1. The ears should be wiped out after every bath or swim to help them dry faster. Use a soft cloth, not a cotton swab.
2. Long hairs under the earflap near the ear canal should be trimmed, again to allow the ears to dry faster. If your dog swims a lot, clip the hair on his head

BE AWARE!

Trim the hair on your dog's feet, especially between his pads, to reduce ice balls in the winter and muddy footprints in the summer. Use scissors and cut the hair even with the pads. Ice balls will affect the way your dog walks.

A well-groomed Golden is a joy to behold.

and neck where his ears brush against him. Wet ears rubbing on wet skin can produce hot spots. Keep the hair short, and rub it with a towel to encourage it to dry faster.

Monitor any earwax you find in your Golden's ears. Large amounts should be gently removed with a soft cloth, not a cotton swab. Some light brown earwax is normal. However, the ears should have no odor, black waxy deposits, or redness. If they do, see your vet.

EYE CARE

The eyes do not need any special care; they only require observation on your part. If you see anything abnormal, call your vet.

HOW TO CARE FOR THE EYES

1. Look into your dog's eyes every day. Check for tearing, excessive blinking, squinting, oozing, or inflammation. Look for any foreign objects such as grass or grass seed.
2. Look for puffiness that could indicate allergies.
3. Watch how your dog approaches steps in semi-darkness. Dogs with decreased

vision adapt quickly but take steps slower. Check with your vet if this seems to be an issue.

NAIL CARE

Goldens have 16 or 18 toenails that must be cut regularly. (Each paw has four nails, and the front ones can have an extra nail called a dewclaw.) They can be dark or light in color, but they are usually large and thick in size. Many breeders remove the dewclaws in the puppy's first three days of life because they can catch on things and are difficult to trim.

Get your puppy used to nail trimming as soon as possible.

Some dogs don't mind having their nails cut, but most are apprehensive. They don't like to have their feet handled, or they pick up the fear their owners feel when faced with the challenge of cutting toenails. If you are one of those owners, find a groomer who will cut the nails regularly, every three or four weeks. If you are cutting them at home, once a week is a good schedule, but every two or three weeks will do.

Nails that are too long catch in rugs and carpet, and really long nails change the way a dog's foot makes contact with the ground. The pads should touch the ground, not the nails. Neglected dogs have nails that grow around and back into the pads, which affects the gait and is quite painful.

HOW TO TRIM THE NAILS

Start with a nail clipper and a pile of treats.

1. Ask your dog to lie down and give him a treat.
2. Pick up a paw and the clippers. Push on the toe to make the nail stand out. Look for the *quick*, a blood vessel that runs through the middle of the toenail. (It is easier to see from the underside.)
3. Clip the nail just before the quick. If you can't see the quick because of dark nails, clip before the big bend in the toe, even with the pads. Take little pieces off the nail until you learn where your dog's quick is. If you cut just a little bit

off the nails every week, the quick will recede.

4. Offer your Golden a treat after every foot, and talk to him in a soothing voice throughout the process.

Be aware that if you nick the quick, it will bleed. This happens occasionally even when professional groomers cut toenails, but it should not happen every time to every nail. A nicked quick results in a sharp pain, and so the next time you pick up the clippers, your Golden may resist. If you do nick the quick, apply pressure, pack the nail with styptic powder or even cornstarch, and wait for the bleeding to stop. It should only take a few minutes.

Offer your dog treats and do only a few nails at each session at first. Cut the nails on one paw tonight and another one tomorrow. Cut off only the tips of the nails to be sure that you do not nick the quick again until he has built up confidence in you.

Also, be flexible. Some Goldens do not like to lie down and offer up a foot; they prefer to stand. If you have such a dog, it will be easier to cut his nails standing up, picking up a paw like a blacksmith would pick up a horse's hoof.

PROFESSIONAL GROOMING

Golden owners should have the name of a professional groomer they can call on occasion. Even people who groom their own dogs need backup. A professional groomer can step in if you are away for a long period or hospitalized—neighbors or family may offer your dog a home, but may not be willing or know how to groom him. It may be a good idea to have your dog professionally groomed before a high school graduation or wedding party at your house or any other occasion where he may be on display. And in case of disaster—think skunk attack—a professional groomer can be a lifesaver.

As when choosing any professional, look for someone who is safety conscious and shares your philosophy about positive training. A groomer should have clean tools and facilities, be kind to dogs, and know how to handle a dog who doesn't enjoy being groomed.

To find a groomer:
- Ask your vet and breeder for grooming recommendations.
- Ask neighbors who have medium- or large-sized dogs if they would recommend their groomer. Ask other Golden owners at the dog park, vet waiting room, obedience class, or outdoor cafe.
- Go to a local dog show and look for grooming ads, Golden handlers, and Golden owners who might be willing to recommend a groomer.

CHAPTER

6

HEALTH OF YOUR GOLDEN RETRIEVER

An enthusiastic Golden Retriever jumping into a lake or over an agility hurdle is the picture of health. You can nurture that good health by making wise choices in feeding, exercise, and preventive health care.

Like all purebred dogs, Goldens have genetic inclinations for some very serious conditions. However, by purchasing your puppy from a responsible breeder, you can reduce your chances of having a dog who suffers from one of these health problems. Puppy buyers should ask to see heart, eye, and joint health clearances for both of their Golden's parents.

FINDING A VET

Think about hiring a vet the way you would hire a housepainter or a lawyer. Shop around, ask for recommendations, and don't just choose the one closest to your home. Your vet needs to be up to date on canine medicine, but she also needs to be able to talk to you. Also, the vet's office should be busy, but not so busy that you have to wait more than an hour every time you go. She should have a staff you can talk to and that likes your dog. Ideally, she should have a backup vet who fills in when she is away.

The vet should be open to conversation about the frequency of vaccinations. She should also be interested in keeping your dog healthy by talking about food, exercise, and training. She should speak to your dog in a friendly way, and talk to you as an equal. She should not seem rushed and too busy to answer questions, especially at scheduled checkups.

Finding the perfect vet for you and your dog will take some trial and error. The first vet you visit may not be right for you. Ask dog owners everywhere you go who they recommend. Check with your breeder or rescue group as well. Listen to what they say—especially people with big dogs—and choose a vet who matches your needs.

THE ANNUAL VET VISIT

After your puppy has grown up, he will have an annual physical exam. Sometimes you will be asked to bring a stool sample. Collect a fresh sample the same day as the vet visit. Use a zip lock bag or a small plastic bottle with a tight lid. Whatever you use should be clean. (And you don't have to bring in the whole stool—just a medium-sized sample.)

Your Golden should be excited to be at the vet's because the people are friendly and he'll get a treat. Once he is taken into an examination room, he will be weighed. Then the vet tech will ask you a series of questions—how often, how much, and what food he eats; how much exercise and sleep he gets; and

Finding the perfect vet for you and your dog may take some trial and error.

what problems you are having. Now is the time to mention anything you have wondered about. Don't worry—vets and vet techs have heard it all before. The vet tech will tell you what vaccinations are due, and you can ask questions about those too.

Then the vet will come in. She will examine your dog from head to toe, looking at his eyes, ears, teeth, and throat; listen to his heart and lungs and belly noises; and engage him to see if he responds. She will take a blood sample for a heartworm test. The results will be ready before you leave. Again, ask questions if you have them.

When you leave, you should have a clear idea of what the vet thinks about your dog's condition, what vaccinations he's received and what they are for, and when you should come back for the next visit. You should also have a paper record of things such as weight, vaccinations, and heartworm test results.

SPAYING AND NEUTERING

Unless you plan to enter your Golden in conformation shows, spay your female or neuter your male. Show dogs have to be intact because dog shows are competitions in which the best dogs for breeding are chosen. But dogs who spend their lives as companions do not need to be bred to be happy. Breeding Goldens is best left to the experts anyway.

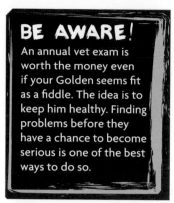

THE BENEFITS

Pet Goldens should be spayed or neutered and will probably be healthier for it. Females especially benefit from spaying—the risk of mammary cancer is reduced to one half of one percent for females spayed before their first heat and to four percent for females spayed after their first heat. For males, neutering reduces the risk of enlarged prostates.

Spayed and neutered Goldens can also be easier to live with. Unspayed females come into season once or twice a year, and they need to be watched around the clock for three weeks so that no unwanted puppies show up. During those three weeks, they have a bloody discharge that can be unpleasant in the house. Unneutered males sometimes go to great lengths to find a female in season, escaping house and yard. They may also be slightly more aggressive toward other males.

WHEN TO SPAY OR NEUTER

Deciding when to spay or neuter your Golden is a question open to debate. Puppy owners will be pressured toward early surgery to eliminate the possibility of unwanted puppies. But recently, the thinking in dog circles is that waiting until Goldens are about a year old may be better for their health—if you are able to manage an intact dog for that many months. The male dog who is 12 or 13 months old and the female who has had one season has had a chance to benefit from hormones that help them achieve full adult growth.

"The risk of some of the common cancers and hip dysplasia increases in dogs spayed or neutered under a year," Rhonda Hovan, Golden breeder and Golden Retriever Club of America (GRCA) health expert, says. A male should reach at least a year of age, she recommends, without question.

THE PROCEDURE

Spaying and neutering is done by a vet under anesthesia. Your dog will have to go without food the night before and the day of the surgery. Both are one-day procedures and do not require overnight stays. Your dog will be ready to go home at the end of the day, a little groggy, with a shaved bald spot.

Goldens recover from spaying and neutering procedures rapidly. They have a high pain tolerance and will want to be back in action sooner than you expect. This means that you have to monitor their activity levels carefully for as many days as your vet recommends. They will need some tender loving care, leash walks, and house rest. Save the dog park for another week.

VACCINATIONS

Vaccinations can save your dog's life by protecting him against diseases that killed dogs for centuries. They will also allow him to take obedience classes, be registered as a therapy dog, travel, and even live in your state. All of these things require one or more vaccinations. In recent years, vaccinations have come under scrutiny by some who say that dogs may be getting vaccine boosters too often. Research is still being done on this topic.

Vaccines called *core vaccines* are those that every puppy should receive. Others, referred to as *noncore vaccines*, may be needed depending on where you live and your dog's lifestyle.

Puppies should get a series of shots between the ages of 6 and 8 weeks and at 16 weeks. Puppy shots given every three to four weeks include the core vaccines against parvovirus, distemper, and adenovirus. The last of those shots should be at about 16 weeks, when the rabies vaccine is also administered. Noncore vaccines are against diseases such as the canine parainfluenza, canine influenza, bordetella, and leptospirosis. Your vet may recommend one of these depending on your puppy's lifestyle (show dogs and dogs frequently boarded usually get a bordetella, or kennel cough, vaccine) or geography.

Pet Goldens should be spayed or neutered.

BORDETELLA

Bordetella, also known as kennel cough, exhibits symptoms such as a distinctive dry cough and runny eyes or nose. Like most respiratory diseases, bordetella can lead to pneumonia, especially in puppies or older dogs. The noncore bordetella vaccine is not required by law but is helpful if you plan to board your dog, show him, or even start regularly attending a doggy day care—all places where he might catch kennel cough from other dogs. The liquid vaccine is dripped into a dog's nose and can be given annually. It is effective, but not a guarantee against all types of kennel cough.

Vaccinations can save your dog's life by protecting him against deadly diseases.

CORONAVIRUS

Coronavirus is an intestinal infection that affects very young puppies. Few vets or vet organizations recommend the noncore vaccination against it because the infection is so mild. Puppies who are kept hydrated and whose diarrhea is controlled recover.

DISTEMPER

Distemper in dogs is a virus related to the measles virus in people. All puppies should receive three vaccinations before 16 weeks of age and one booster a year later. The American Animal Hospital Association (AAHA) recommends re-evaluation and possibly another booster three years later. Sometimes puppies get distemper before they have had all of these core shots. Many cases are mild. In others, the virus first causes fever, a yellow sticky discharge from the eyes and nose, and vomiting and diarrhea. The second stage may include seizures because the virus attacks the brain.

HEARTWORM

Heartworm is a potentially fatal parasite that dogs can get from mosquitoes in all 50 states. The larvae enter the dog's blood, mature, and settle in his heart and lungs. The worms cause fatigue and a cough at first, then weight loss and difficulty breathing. Treatment includes poisoning the worms, usually with arsenic, which can be dangerous for older dogs or dogs in poor condition. It is much better to prevent heartworm in the first place than to try to treat it. The American Heartworm Society (AHS) recommends that all dogs have a blood test for heartworm annually. If the test is negative, your dog can start on a heartworm preventive, usually a monthly pill or topical treatment frequently given year round.

LEPTOSPIROSIS

Leptospirosis is spread by the urine of an infected animal. A dog gets it by drinking or swimming in water that contains the bacteria. Symptoms include fever, vomiting, weakness, and refusal to eat. Treatment starts with an antibiotic and may proceed to dialysis. People can get leptospirosis from infected dogs, although the risk is low.

This vaccine is considered noncore. Your vet can help you decide if your Golden needs it based on outbreaks in your area or if you live in an area populated by rats and mice that may carry the bacteria. The AAHA recommends that the vaccine be given to puppies older than 12 weeks.

It's easier to prevent heartworm than to cure it.

PARVOVIRUS

Parvovirus is a core vaccine that is given in three doses to all puppies between 6 and 16 weeks of age. A booster is given a year later and again three years later. Dogs get parvo from infected feces, such as when a puppy walks through another dog's feces at a dog park and then licks his feet. Parvo causes severe intestinal upset; puppies vomit and have diarrhea until they are in danger of dehydration. Most cases occur in puppies five months old or younger.

RABIES

Rabies is a fatal disease that a dog can get from wildlife in your backyard (such as skunks, bats, coyotes, and raccoons) and give to you. All states require rabies vaccination, a core vaccine, for dogs. Typically, puppies are vaccinated at 16 weeks, given a booster a year later, and then in many states, administered boosters every three years after that. If your dog is scratched or bitten by a wild animal, call your vet. She will probably want to thoroughly clean the wound, revaccinate him, and keep a close eye on him for about six weeks.

PARASITES

The battle against parasites—creatures that live off your dog—is unending. These creatures range from parasites that are so tiny you can't see them to those big enough to pinch between your fingers. They all annoy your dog, and some can cause serious harm to his health. Fortunately, we have an arsenal of tools against parasites.

EXTERNAL PARASITES

External parasites are those that attack your dog's coat and skin.

Fleas

Fleas are the original bloodsuckers. They jump onto your dog, bite into him, and feast on his blood. A few fleabites will make him scratch, but hundreds or thousands of fleas can do serious damage, especially to a puppy, who may become anemic. But it gets worse. Some dogs develop an allergy to flea saliva and start scratching furiously. Some fleas carry other parasites, such as tapeworms.

Watch for fleas on your Golden's head, where the hair is shorter. Dark brown fleas are easy to spot in his coat as they jump from place to place. Also look for "flea dirt," or feces, on your Golden's back, near his tail. Flea eggs appear as small white grains on your dog before falling off. Flea eggs also hide in carpeting, in cracks in the floor, and in furniture, where they live to fight another day.

Flea control must include both the dog and his environment. Start by shampooing your dog in a shower where the fleas will drown and be washed down the drain before they have a chance to climb back on. Also, wash all bedding in hot water. If your dog had a bad flea infestation, you may have to use an insecticide to get rid of flea eggs in the house or yard.

Your vet can help you pick a topical flea treatment that you apply to your dog's back that will kill adult fleas almost immediately. Then, you

Dog Tale

My dog Bailey could eat a whole dish of kibble and leave behind the heartworm pill I threw in. I had to give it to her wrapped in peanut butter and bread.

Check your Golden for fleas and ticks after he's been outdoors.

give your dog a monthly treatment that will stop the fleas from reproducing. This is a one-two punch that will kill live fleas and their future offspring.

The good news is that you can avoid almost all of this by picking a heartworm preventive—oral or topical—that also includes a flea-controlling substance.

Mites

Mites are microscopic creatures that live on your dog's skin or in his ears. They cause itching and mange, an uneven coat with irritated skin underneath. Many different types of mites love to live on dogs. With scabies, for example, female mites burrow under a dog's skin to lay eggs. The dog scratches, his hair falls out, and the skin becomes inflamed. Scabies is contracted from other dogs and contaminated grooming equipment. Chiggers are another type of mite that your dog might find on a hike in the woods or fields. They cluster on thin skin— between the toes or near the mouth.

Mites are easily treatable with prescription medication.

Ringworm

Ringworm is a fungus that looks like a circle of irritated and bald skin with a red perimeter; it may itch if infected by bacteria. Your dog can get it from the hair of infected dogs left behind on carpeting or stuck in a hairbrush. Or he can get it from you—and you can get it from him.

This is a very treatable disease, but treatment takes four to six weeks. The skin can be treated with an antifungal cream administered twice daily. If the dog has several affected sites, a prescription drug can be given orally. Remove as much hair as possible from your home, and wash all grooming equipment to prevent reinfection.

Ticks

Ticks vary in size, from the size of a pinhead to the size of a pea. They carry several diseases, including Lyme disease and Rocky Mountain spotted fever. Ticks jump onto a dog from long grasses and plants and stay there for several days, drinking blood and swelling.

If you find a tick stuck on your dog, don't squeeze it; people can get several of the diseases that ticks carry. Wear rubber gloves and pull the tick off with tweezers. Drop it into rubbing alcohol to kill it. Many ticks can survive being flushed down the toilet, so skip that disposal method. Then, spread antibiotic ointment on the bite site. Call your vet to see which tick-borne diseases are possible in your area. Ask if she wants to identify the tick before you toss it.

Some monthly heartworm and flea treatments also kill ticks, but not all do. That's why it's important to read labels. Most importantly, check your dog for ticks after every run through woods or fields.

INTERNAL PARASITES

Internal parasites are those that attack the inside of your Golden's body.

Heartworms

Heartworms are 4- to 12-inch-long (10- to 30.5-cm) worms that live in a dog's lungs and heart. They enter his bloodstream as larvae when he is bitten by an infected mosquito. The dog first appears to tire easily and cough. Then he starts to lose weight, cough even more, and breathe rapidly. Untreated dogs can have up to 250 worms, a number sufficient to kill a dog.

The sooner the worms are discovered, the easier the treatment will be. Heartworm is treated with drugs that contain arsenic, a poison that can be hard on very young and very old dogs. The disease is easily prevented with a monthly prescription drug and annual blood test.

Hookworms

Hookworms grow rapidly in warm, humid conditions. They attach themselves to the small intestine and suck blood. Less than 1/2 inch (1.5 cm) long, they can cause severe blood loss and malnutrition.

Puppies can get hookworms through the placenta before they are born or from their mother's milk. Dogs can get hookworms by eating or licking soil or anything else contaminated by worms left there in feces. A hookworm can even hook itself through the pawpads.

Symptoms include dark diarrhea, pale gums, weight loss, and weakness. Thorough cleanup of a sick puppy's yard must be done to prevent recontamination. Fortunately, some heartworm preventives also prevent hookworms.

Roundworms

Roundworms are quite common in puppies and dogs. Puppies get the worms through the placenta or their mother's milk. Dogs can lick or eat something contaminated by the worms or their eggs. Occasionally, a dog will even eat a mouse that has roundworms and become contaminated in that way.

Roundworms are a common internal parasite in puppies.

Roundworms form cysts in adult dogs and become harmless, but in puppies the parasites cause diarrhea, anemia, and potbellies. Roundworms are easily treated with dewormers and some heartworm preventives. Humans can pick up roundworms too, so all surfaces that a sick puppy touches must be thoroughly cleaned.

Tapeworms

Tapeworms are an intestinal parasite that can grow several feet (m) long. A tapeworm has a head that sucks blood from a dog and a body made up of white segments that break off. You can see them in feces or on your dog's rear end.

Dogs get tapeworms by licking itchy fleas that carry tapeworm eggs and swallowing them. When you see anything that looks like white rice in your Golden's hair or in his feces, call your vet. Tapeworms are easily treated.

Whipworms

Whipworms are thin and only a couple of inches (cm) long. One end is thicker than the other, making them resemble whips. They attach themselves to the intestines and suck a dog's blood, causing diarrhea.

Whipworms need to be treated two or three times before they are eliminated. See your vet for medications. Some heartworm preventives also prevent whipworms.

GOLDEN RETRIEVER HEALTH PROBLEMS

Like all purebred dogs, Golden Retrievers began in a small gene pool. As breeders specialized, many used only a few prize-winning males and relied on line-breeding (breeding close relatives) to establish their look. Any genetics faults, then, were magnified many times, creating health problems that continue to ripple through the breed.

Today, Golden lovers are concerned about high rates of cancer and eye issues that lead to blindness only in Golden Retrievers.

The Golden Retriever Club of America recommends buying a puppy only from a breeder whose dogs have passed eye, hip, elbow, and heart health tests. Those are four common genetic flaws that Goldens pass down from generation to generation. The good news is, with consistent testing, and by breeding only dogs who have passed the tests, these flaws can and have been reduced. But the bad news is that two parents whose hips have passed the test, for example, can still produce puppies who have hip dysplasia. The odds are reduced but not eliminated.

ALLERGIES

Allergies can be caused by something a dog eats, breathes in, or touches. Dogs can be allergic to any single ingredient in dog food, and pinpointing an allergen can be a hit-or-miss, trial-and-error process. Goldens can be allergic to seasonal things like grass or trees, or everyday things like wool blankets, plastic dishes, or dust mites.

Dogs with allergies itch, have red skin, lick their feet, and may have runny eyes and noses. They may lick or scratch themselves so much that they develop a hot spot—a bald patch of skin that is irritated and usually infected. This requires a vet's attention. Goldens have a reputation for getting more than the usual number of hot spots, but not all Goldens do. Some will have only two or three in a lifetime.

Dogs with mild seasonal allergies may benefit from antihistamines. Your vet will advise you about a safe medication for your dog.

CANCER

Cancer kills more Goldens than any other disease—60 percent of all Goldens. That is almost double the cancer rate in all dogs, according to Golden breeder and GRCA health expert Rhonda Hovan. The two types of cancer most common in Goldens are hemangiosarcoma in the blood vessel cells and lymphosarcoma in the lymph system.

Vets should always check out lumps or lack of appetite, two main symptoms of cancer. Other symptoms include lethargy, pale gums, weight loss, and difficulty breathing.

The good news is that research into dog cancer has exploded, partly because dogs and humans get many of the same types of cancer, and partly because dogs today are seen as part of the family. As a result, treatment has advanced dramatically. Dogs with cancer can sometimes benefit from drugs and surgery that will prolong their life. Major veterinary schools have oncology departments that can run tests and possibly enroll your dog in a study.

The GRCA Golden Retriever Foundation and the Morris Animal Foundation are working to answer the question: Why do so many Goldens get cancer? Their MADGiC Project (Making Advanced Discoveries in Golden Cancers) is one of

Good breeders are trying to reduce the occurrence of hip dysplasia in the breed.

several examples of major scientific research going on in canine cancer. But if you have a dog diagnosed with cancer, that may be small consolation. Other Golden owners may have a dog diagnosed with cancer and will understand the depth of your emotion. Reach out for support.

EYE PROBLEMS

Goldens can inherit several eye problems, including cataracts and problems with the retina and eyelid or eyelashes. Pigmentary uveitis, an eye defect that has been found in higher numbers recently in Goldens, leads to glaucoma and blindness. Its cause and treatment are still being researched, but the Pittsburgh Veterinary Specialty and Emergency Center says that the cause is most likely an inherited autoimmune disorder, treated with surgery and long-term medications. But treatment is frequently not effective.

Puppies should come from two parents who have passed an annual eye test given by a canine ophthalmologist affiliated with the Canine Eye Registry Foundation (CERF).

HIP DYSPLASIA

Hip dysplasia is a joint problem that affects about 30 percent of Golden Retrievers. It can be mild or severe. This genetic condition can be made worse by poor diet and excessive exercise in a puppy's first year.

In a dog with hip dysplasia, the bones in the hip joint don't fit together tightly. They eventually wear down, and the dog gets painful arthritis. Overweight dogs put more stress on the lax joint, and puppies who have had a high-calorie diet grow faster than their joints can handle. Puppies who are asked to jog or jump hurdles sometimes get a more serious case of dysplasia.

Symptoms to watch for are puppies younger than a year old with a limp in their back legs, inability to jump into the car, and using the back legs to hop rather than run. Treatment includes pain medication, glucosamine, and sometimes surgery.

Elbow dysplasia is a similar condition, affecting the joints on the front legs of about 12 percent of Goldens. Puppies limp, favoring their front leg instead of the rear. Surgery is the cure.

HEART DEFECTS

Heart defects can be very serious in Golden Retrievers. One of the first symptoms is tiring easily during exercise with labored breathing. Some heart problems Goldens get include subvalvular aortic stenosis (SAS), arrhythmias, and cardiomyopathy.

In SAS, the valves narrow, creating a murmur as the heart works harder. Other symptoms include coughing, rapid breathing, and shortness of breath. Beta blockers, medication prescribed by your vet to slow your Golden's heart rate, are the most effective treatment. Surgery has been less successful. An arrhythmia is an irregularity in the dog's heartbeat caused by a problem in his electrical circuit that can lead to death. Your vet will try to determine what is causing the irregular heartbeat and prescribe medication. In dilated cardiomyopathy, the dog's heart muscles weaken and thin. Several types of medication are possible, including Digitalis (to increase the force of the heart contractions and slow them down), diuretics (to reduce fluid), and ACE inhibitors (to dilate the blood vessels). Goldens can drop dead from heart defects at a young age.

HYPOTHYROIDISM

Thyroid problems are easy to diagnose—they require only a blood test—and treat. Hypothyroidism is a hormone deficiency that causes hair loss, a dull coat, weight gain, cold intolerance, and lethargy. Dogs treated with thyroid hormone once or twice a day may appear to be experiencing a miracle because their symptoms disappear, but they must be treated for life. Thyroid dosage requires monitoring by a vet and regular retesting.

ALTERNATIVE THERAPIES

Many Golden ailments respond to alternative therapies—treatments not traditionally taught in a college of veterinary medicine. Alternative therapies usually take more time to work than traditional medical or surgical options.

ACUPUNCTURE

Acupuncture has become more accepted as a treatment for the symptoms of canine arthritis, and is also used for some skin, gastrointestinal, reproductive, and respiratory problems. It involves slender needles

Alternative therapies can be used in conjunction with traditional veterinary medicine.

slid into the dog's skin to stimulate nerves and increase circulation. Acupuncture is safe when performed by a trained acupuncturist. Your vet may be able to recommend a veterinary acupuncturist.

CHIROPRACTIC

Chiropractic practitioners specialize in adjusting the spinal vertebrae and the joints. Veterinary specialists will work to alleviate pain, muscle spasms, eating problems, and bowel or bladder disorders, but they often see themselves as working with a traditional vet rather than in place of one. Look for someone licensed by the American Veterinary Chiropractic Association (AVCA).

HERBAL

Herbal medicine is one of the oldest alternative therapies. It has come back into popularity, but carries a few caveats for dog owners. Herbs have side effects, and before giving one to your dog, research side effects on dogs and potential interactions with anything else he is taking. Ask for specifics on what benefits an herb offers, and research the backing on that claim.

The US federal government does not regulate herbs, and the exact content of a bottle is not guaranteed. Still, some herbs are useful, such as cranberry for canine urinary problems. In addition, ginger (in the form of gingersnaps) can be helpful for dogs with upset stomachs.

HOLISTIC

The American Holistic Veterinary Medical Association (AHVMA) defines holistic medicine as "the examination and diagnosis of an animal, considering all aspects of the animal's life and employing all of the practitioner's senses, as well as the combination of conventional and alternative (or complementary) modalities of treatment." So, a holistic veterinarian will ask more questions about your Golden's behaviors, medical and dietary history, and things such as stress. Holistic vets are less invasive than traditional vets and willingly use alternative treatments such as acupuncture and herbs.

FIRST AID

Goldens are impulsive, energetic dogs. Sometimes they get hurt. They get a thorn in their paw, a nail ripped off, a bee sting, a wound from a downed tree, or an upset stomach from eating something they dug up. It's up to you to help your dog until you can get to a professional.

Plan for emergencies as if you know they will happen. Keep your vet's telephone number on speed dial. Assemble a first-aid kit that includes a flashlight, tweezers, scissors, bandaging materials such as gauze pads and surgical tape, antibiotic ointment, saline eye wash, and Betadine antiseptic scrub. Compile a list of emergency phone numbers, such as a 24-hour vet clinic near you that takes emergencies and the ASPCA Poison Control number—(888) 426-4435. The ASPCA charges a consultation fee.

In any emergency, stay calm, try to observe the details (did the dog who bit yours have a collar? a license tag?), and collect any evidence a vet might find useful. Use socks or scarves to tie around your dog's mouth if pain has made him snappish.

BITES

If your dog gets bit by a strange dog, stop the bleeding with pressure and a clean cloth. Ask about the dog who bit yours—licensed or stray? Wrap the bite and head for the vet's immediately.

BURNS

If your dog is burned, cover the burned skin with wet gauze and go immediately to a vet.

FROSTBITE AND HEATSTROKE

Keep an eye on your dog on the hottest and coldest days. Frostbite requires a warm—not hot—bath. Heatstroke requires swift treatment: a cooling mist, a cool towel, cool water to drink, and air-conditioning. Both need veterinary attention.

POISONING

The ASPCA's website—www.aspca.org—has a list of poisonous plants, and as mentioned earlier, a Poison Control number to call. It recommends collecting a sample of whatever your dog ate to take with you to the vet.

SENIOR DOGS

The Golden life span is between 10 and 13 years, but some Goldens today live to be 14 or 15. The old Golden is a wise senior citizen who has left all the puppy nonsense behind. He will be happy to see you, he will be eager to eat, and he will be able to go on walks, but he will also understand things a puppy never can. You can connect on new levels with your old dog—much deeper and more satisfying levels.

Goldens are considered senior dogs around eight years of age.

Dogs age at different rates. Some Goldens will achieve a slower steadiness as early as five or six, and others not until nine or ten. White hair on the face has no correlation to health. Goldens are officially "senior" by age eight, although some dogs don't show any signs. Sometime after his eighth birthday—maybe not until his ninth or tenth—start scheduling vet checkups twice a year. Ask if he needs as many vaccination boosters as usual. Watch for signs of aging, such as arthritis, cataracts, or canine cognitive disorder (CCD), which is similar to Alzheimer's in people. Its symptoms are confusion and failure to recognize people or places.

Keep track of your dog's weight. If he has slowed down, he may not need as much food. Talk to your vet about senior foods or weight-control diets. It may be that all you have to do is cut down on the amount of his familiar food and give fewer treats. But cherish your dog and improve the quality of his treats. For example, offer him cooked salmon or chicken as a treat instead of biscuits. This is a time to celebrate.

Start protecting your Golden from himself. Don't allow strenuous physical activity to continue for hours. He may not know when it is time to quit, so you must be the one to put away the tennis ball or pack up and leave the beach. But don't give up on exercise. Even dogs with arthritis can benefit from leisurely leash walks. Old dogs can even learn new tricks. Go slowly and use your Golden's favorite treats, and see how pleased he will be with himself.

The sad fact of life with dogs is that they have a much shorter life than we have. If your Golden gets cancer or severe hip dysplasia, your vet can help you decide when it is time to end his life painlessly and quickly. What no one can tell you ahead of time is how much you will miss your Golden. For some people, only another Golden will help, while for others, no dog can replace the one they lost and they choose to go dogless. This is a personal decision. But most people will tell you that it is better to have known the love of a Golden and suffer the sadness when he leaves than to never have known the joy he brought to your life.

TRAINING YOUR
GOLDEN RETRIEVER

Your dream dog isn't born that way. One of the biggest myths about owning a Golden Retriever is that he walks into your life practically perfect in every way. In fact, Goldens have to learn what you want. And before that, they have to learn the words—the actual language—they need to understand you. Finally, they have to develop the self-control to become a member of the family. Like anything else, those behaviors come with time and practice. That's where you and a good dog training class come in.

WHY TRAIN YOUR GOLDEN?

Goldens are 65 to 75 pounds (29.5 to 34 kg) of boundless enthusiasm, driven by sharp intelligence and keen instincts. If you don't train them to do what *you* want, they will do what *they* want, energetically and impulsively. That can include stealing food from the table, chewing throw rugs, leaping on furniture, and jumping up on people to lick their faces. They are big enough to cause big trouble.

But with consistency and patience on your part, most Goldens will learn fast—faster than some other breeds. Goldens are hardwired to please their owners. They were bred in Scotland to work closely with a human, hunting and retrieving game as a team. They had to be biddable. That is why they are determined to please you, the most important living creature in their life, their team leader.

"Most of everything you hear [that's] good about Goldens is true," says Teresa Campbell, Maryland breeder. "They are family dogs, very intelligent. They are a people dog. They need to be with people."

And so the real reason to train your Golden is to experience the most satisfying relationship you can with him. A well-trained dog trusts you, understands and even anticipates what you want, looks to you for direction, and is willing to cooperate. He is your partner. He is able to have a deep and lasting relationship with a human. And isn't that why you got a dog in the first place?

POSITIVE TRAINING

Positive dog training rewards the good things your dog does instead of punishing the bad. It helps build a strong relationship between you and your dog—quickly. You are the source of praise and treats and tennis balls and whatever other rewards you choose.

Positive training works especially well with the sensitive Golden. Shouting at them when they do something wrong can slow down training and instill fear and suspicion in them. Most are food oriented and will work for the tiniest treat. They are willing to please, and they will offer you several options if they are not sure what you want—sit, down, roll over. They will try them all until they figure out what you want. Most of them enjoy that mental exercise in the same way many people enjoy a crossword puzzle. When they get it right and you respond with praise, you can almost see them thinking, "Aha, so that's what she wants." The mental exercise in positive training is good for Goldens. These smart dogs enjoy learning new words and behaviors and thrive on stimulation.

HELP YOUR DOG SUCCEED

Positive dog trainers look for ways to help a dog succeed and avoid situations that might set him up for failure. A dog fails when there are too many distractions or when you ask him to do something he doesn't understand. This is why it's important to break a new command into easy steps; ask him to sit before you teach him the down, for example.

If you are teaching your dog to sit, positive training tells you to lure him into position with food held over his nose and moved backward. He will sit to get the food, you enthusiastically praise and treat him, and he remembers that you did so. This was a good experience for him, and he will learn to sit quickly.

IGNORE INCORRECT BEHAVIORS

If for some reason he doesn't sit the first time, positive training teaches you to ignore him, do something else for a minute, and then try again. In positive training, no one shouts at the dog, hits him, or jerks him into a sit. The idea is to get the dog to do what you want him to do on his own, and then reward him profusely. But no reward is given to the dog who doesn't cooperate. You ignore him, which is the hard part. Goldens have big brown eyes that beg eloquently for food and attention. The temptation is to throw him the food even if he didn't do what you want and just end the training session. But don't reward noncompliance, not even once.

ESTABLISH A ROUTINE

Positive training is easier if it is incorporated into a well-established routine. If

Most Goldens are food oriented and will work for the tiniest treat.

you do the same things every day in the same order, your dog will pick up on the routine very quickly. He will learn good behavior in spite of himself. If, for example, you expect him to sit before you put the food down, and you hold the dish and wait until he sits, soon he will sit as soon as you pour the food into the dish. He will be trained without a harsh word. When strangers want to give him a treat, he will be much more inclined to sit and wait for the treat because he has learned that good things happen when he sits. Soon you will have a well-trained dog.

SOCIALIZATION

"Socialization" is a fancy word for talking to your dog, taking him places, and introducing him to new things when he is young. The typical Golden owner wants a dog she can take to the park, to the outdoor cafe, to the beach, and on a walk along a city sidewalk. She wants a dog she can enter in canine sporting events, one who will ignore the other dogs and focus on the competition. She wants a nice dog who is friendly and outgoing, a dog who doesn't growl or snap at people. That takes socialization.

HOW TO SOCIALIZE

The socialized dog has learned the ins and outs of the world he lives in and is not afraid of life. Dogs who live in fear sometimes do antisocial things such as bark or lunge.

Socialize your Golden in his first year—or even better, in his first six months—to learn that babies in strollers are not going to hurt him. Teach him that wheelchairs are no big deal, that cats can be tolerated, and that traffic can be ignored. Most importantly, teach him that other dogs on leashes are not a threat and that new people are probably going to be nice to him. Have him meet people of both genders, all ages and heights, and people wearing hats and coats that are big and billowy.

Fortunately, Golden puppies are so cute that they are easy to socialize. Strangers will want to pet your dog, and some will want to hold him. Soon your puppy will learn that a wide variety of people are friendly and nonthreatening. If you take him to all the places you will go when he is an adult, he will learn what to expect and how to behave.

If you have a young adult dog, you can still work on socialization. It just may take longer and require you to go more slowly. Dogs who are not used to children, for example, may become overwhelmed in a large group of children. Introduce your Golden to one child for limited playtime if this is the case with him.

A well-socialized Golden takes meeting new people and encountering new things in his stride.

In your favor is the fact that most Goldens like people. "Usually, socializing a Golden is easy—a good Golden seems to be 'preprogrammed' for such," says Marcia Schlehr, Golden breeder and historian.

Of course, all Goldens are not identical. Each dog is different. Some take to children more easily than others. Some will never like loud noises. A few will even bristle at the sight of another dog long after he should have learned to trust the person on the end of the leash. That's where teamwork comes in. You are your dog's teammate, and it is up to you to know what his limits are. Sometimes it is better to avoid the risk of a dog bite by avoiding situations that upset your dog.

CRATE TRAINING

The idea of putting a puppy in a crate upsets some new Golden owners. He is so cute and so cuddly that they don't want to put him a "cage" like a zoo animal. They see their dog sleeping in front of the fire, a member of the family. But he is a puppy, recently removed from his mother and siblings, a puppy who doesn't know the house, the house rules, or even the people in the house. He is a baby. He needs a place where he can feel safe, a place that is his, and a place where he can turn "off."

WHY USE A CRATE?

As puppies, Goldens are very curious and can get into life-threatening trouble if left out in the house alone. They learn by putting everything in their mouth— socks, soap, toilet paper, coins, and electrical cords. In a crate, they are safe from their own curiosity. So think of the crate as a safe and cozy den similar to the place in which wolves choose to raise their pups.

Safety and security may be the two biggest reasons to use a crate, but the third is very practical: Crate training is the easiest way to housetrain a puppy. Most dogs do not want to soil their "nest" and will hold it until you take them outside. Of course, there are exceptions and sometimes brand-new puppies do not recognize a strange crate as theirs on the first day. At other times, a puppy left in a crate too long just can't hold it and will use a far corner in which to eliminate. But for most Goldens, crate training is efficient and easy.

CRATE LOCATION

A crate should be close enough to the family so that the puppy can hear household noises. A basement or garage is too isolated. A better choice is a spare bathroom, a corner of the bedroom or living room, an unused dining room, or a mudroom. Covering the crate increases the den feeling, heightening your puppy's sense of security, and reduces the distractions visible to him.

HOW TO CRATE TRAIN

Place your puppy in his crate for short periods at first, gradually getting to the point where he can sleep through the night. If you have a large crate that will fit an adult Golden, block off most of it so that the puppy only has a small space that's big enough to stand up and turn around in—you don't want him to be able to eliminate in a far corner. Feed him in the crate to help him see it as his den. Good things happen in his crate.

You also want your puppy to be able to sleep through the night in his crate. Goldens were meant to be energetic dogs in the field, with the ability to relax and live in the house with their upper-class Scottish families. They should have an "off" switch, and helping your dog develop it is part of your job. This is why bedtime is a good concept for your dog to know. It is when everybody—dogs and people—sleeps for a long stretch. No food. No attention. No expectations. The dog learns that when he is put in the crate at the end of the day, he can relax and sleep. He has no responsibilities. It is part of a routine that makes him feel safe.

After he is housetrained, your dog should still sleep in the crate at night for some months for his own safety. Golden puppies may chew well into their

A crate is a place where your Golden can feel safe.

second year. After a few months, you can buy a cheap fleece or artificial lambskin to replace the towel and eventually move up to a crate pad. You can also leave the crate door open in the daytime and be surprised when your older puppy goes into the crate for a nap—with the door open.

As long as your puppy does not spend 24 hours a day in his crate, he will learn to love it and feel secure. It is his place, and he'll feel at home in it.

HOUSETRAINING

Most Goldens learn housetraining in a short time—a couple of months at most. Many learn more quickly, and of course, a few are slower. In the end, all healthy adult Goldens on a well-planned schedule rarely have accidents in the house. But even with an able learner, housetraining a puppy takes some hard work on your part.

HOW TO HOUSETRAIN

The secrets to successful housetraining are routine, positive feedback, confinement, and alertness.

Follow a Routine

Routine is a very important part of housetraining. Your puppy's day should be scheduled, and it should be the same every day—at least for the first few

Routine is a very important part of housetraining.

months. That way, he'll know what you expect. He should eat and immediately go out at the same times every day. His exercise time and playtime should end with time outside before he is put into his crate for a nap. The schedule should

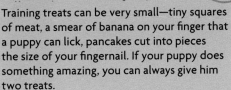

PUPPY POINTER

Training treats can be very small—tiny squares of meat, a smear of banana on your finger that a puppy can lick, pancakes cut into pieces the size of your fingernail. If your puppy does something amazing, you can always give him two treats.

be set up with an understanding of what he is physically able to do. An eight- or nine-week-old puppy, for example, can't stay in a crate for eight or nine hours while his family is at work. Someone must come home at lunch or after school to let the puppy out every day for a few weeks. A friend or neighbor might be able to help out.

Puppies who are not housetrained should sleep in a crate that is only big enough for them to stand up and turn around in. In the morning, open the crate when your puppy is quiet and still. Wait until he stops barking or jumping. This is an important part of the routine that should start the first day you bring him home.

Carry your puppy outside immediately to a grassy spot you have chosen as his potty spot and say a potty command ("Go potty" or "Take care of business" or even "Hurry up"). Wait until he urinates. Get excited and praise him, and play with him a little. Then take him back in and feed him in the crate. As soon as he finishes, take him out to the same spot, say the potty command, and wait until he defecates. Praise him profusely. Then you can play with him for a longer time.

If you always take him out when you open the crate and before you put him back in, he will learn to hold his urine when he is in the crate. Soon he will be able to make it through the night, and as he grows into an adult, he will make it through the workday.

Remember to stay with your puppy when he is outside, and be alert. Watch him carefully. This is not the time to check your text messages or even talk on the phone. You must make sure that he urinates every time, and praise him before you go back inside.

Take your puppy out for the last time as late as you can—11 p.m. or even midnight—at first, and plan to be up as early as 6 a.m. Gradually, your puppy will grow into a more human schedule.

Praise Enthusiastically

The feedback for your puppy eliminating outside has to be immediate, enthusiastic, and noisy. Make it a party every time he eliminates outside. Golden owners get used to clapping and excitedly saying "Good dog!" even at 11 p.m. The puppy, after all, is too young to know words, so he is looking for other signs that you are happy. Be happy. Make him feel like he did something important and good so that he wants to do it again.

Confine Your Puppy

Confine your untrained puppy to a room with a floor that is easily cleaned, such as the kitchen. Some Golden owners will tell you that their dog had no accidents when

If your puppy is signaling that he has to go potty, take him outside to his designated area.

he was a puppy, but take those stories with a grain of salt. Puppies have accidents. Keep a roll of paper towels and an enzyme spray cleaner that removes odors handy. Puppies are attracted to places that smell like they have been used before, so it's important to clean up accidents quickly and thoroughly.

Confining a puppy to a kitchen is not animal cruelty. It is a safety issue. It is easier to keep an eye on him if he is allowed access to only one room. To a small puppy, a kitchen is a large space and one that he can explore and learn before he is introduced to other rooms. Soon, the kitchen will start to seem like his den and he will be reluctant to soil it.

Remain Alert

When in the house, keep an eye on your puppy and watch for signs that he has to go out. Puppies will start to look for a good spot, nose down, circling. If your dog is doing this, pick him up immediately and take him outside. Say your potty word or phrase and watch and wait.

Puppies will have to go out more frequently when they are playing and exercising. An older puppy may go to the door and look back at you. When that begins to happen, it is important to respond immediately so that he learns that he can tell you something and you can be counted on to reply. Understanding when he has to go out will help him have fewer and eventually no accidents in the house.

BASIC COMMANDS

Teaching your dog basic commands—*sit, come, stay, down,* and *heel*—is a good idea. Goldens like a challenge, and learning a new behavior keeps them mentally sharp. Following a command teaches your dog that you are in charge and that he should pay attention to you. It can also improve your relationship. Finally, the basic commands will allow your dog to fit into human society and go more places. They may even save his life someday.

When teaching the basic commands, keep practice sessions short. Goldens are smart and get bored quickly. It is better to have two short sessions in a day than one long one.

SIT

The *sit* is a good command to start with. Very young puppies can be taught to sit, and that action can stop negative behavior without any punitive undertones. For example, a puppy who is caught rummaging through a wastebasket can be told to sit and then praised while the wastebasket is taken away. No negative words need be spoken.

Training a puppy to sit requires a *lure,* a food that's attractive to your puppy, such as cooked chicken. You could use puppy kibble, at least at first, but a highly desirable food makes the process faster and more fun for a puppy.

How to Teach It

1. While your puppy is standing in front of you, hold a small piece of food right above his nose.
2. Slowly move the food up just a bit and back. The puppy will sit to keep an eye on the food.
3. Give him the food as soon as he sits. Be happy—say "Good dog" with enthusiasm. After he does it a few times, start using the word "sit."

After your dog learns the basics, reinforce the command by asking him to sit before you put his food dish down, before you open the crate, before you open any door, before you put his leash on, and before you offer him any treat.

Each time he sits, be sure to give a *release* command so that he knows when he can stand up again. You can pick any word or phrase—"release," "free," "free dog,"

Hold a treat over your Golden's nose to teach him the sit.

"okay"—as long as you use it consistently so that your dog knows you no longer expect him to sit.

COME (RECALL)

Many trainers say that the *come* command is the most important. If a dog slips out of the house or the car and takes off, this command may be the only thing between him and calamity. If your dog is in a fenced area, and you see a skunk or porcupine coming, the *come* command can prove its worth. But it can be a little harder to teach than the *sit*.

How to Teach It

The first step is to pick a word. You can use any word or phrase, as long as you use the same one every time and don't use it for anything else. It could be "come," "front" (as in come and sit in front of me), "here," or "by me" (come back and stay by me). Everyone in the house must use the same word and be prepared to reward your dog richly when he responds.

Also, to entice your dog to come to you, you have to outshine all the distractions along the way. And you have to be an attractive goal. Why should your dog give up chasing that squirrel if he knows that you are going to scold him when he shows up? So drop any thoughts of an angry scene with your runaway dog. If he comes back when you call him, praise him for coming back. No harsh words about running away in the first place. Feed him several tasty treats, and this time it has to be something better than kibble. This calls for a high-value treat that your dog will remember the next time he is running and you call him.

Teaching the *come* goes faster with two people:

1. Have your friend hold your dog while you move away, carrying some chicken the dog has seen.
2. Turn and call him. He will come barreling at you to get the chicken.
3. Tell him that he is the smartest dog ever, and give him two or three bites of chicken.
4. Move farther and farther away each time until he has to run past several interesting things to get to you. Each time he does, reward him lavishly.
5. After a couple of times, ask him to sit before you give him the treat.

Another way to teach the come is to have two people in different rooms or outside on different sides of a house, out of sight of each other. Each is loaded with a highly desirable food, such as small bits of hotdog. They take turns calling the dog to them, rewarding and praising him when he comes and saying nothing if he doesn't come.

Always praise your dog for coming to you.

STAY

A dog who knows the *stay* command will stay in the car when you open the door, remain on the examining table at the vet's, and keep still while you groom him. He is dog who has good manners and can go places with the family. However, teaching the *stay* can take some time. Puppies have short attention spans and may forget that you told them to stay.

The *stay* comes in three varieties—*sit, stand,* and *down*—but all are taught in the same way.

How to Teach It

1. Start with your dog sitting in front of you and a highly desirable reward in your hand, such as half a banana.
2. Say "Stay" and take a step backward. If your dog remains in place, step forward and feed him the treat and praise him. If he follows you, don't reward or praise him; just put him back where he was and try again.
3. If he stays in place, repeat the command once or twice, and then try two steps and then three.
4. Use the *release* command to end the exercise and indicate to your dog that he is free to get out of the *stay*. You should be the one who decides when he can move.

The *down* should be taught after your dog knows the *sit* command.

GOLDEN RETRIEVER

BE AWARE!

A very young puppy should not be allowed to go up or down stairs. Stairs are dangerous places that puppies can easily fall down and hurt themselves. Once on another floor, out of sight, puppies can find things, such as prescription medicines, full wastebaskets, laundry soaps, and dirty clothes. Baby gates should be used for at least a few weeks to keep him confined and out of trouble.

Practice only a few times in each session at first if you have a young puppy, and always go back a level if he attempts to follow you. For example, if you have made it to three steps but your puppy gets up to follow, go back to two steps a couple of times.

Eventually, you should be able to get to the other side of the room, walking away with your back to your puppy. This doesn't happen in a week, and it won't happen at all with a nine-week-old puppy, but if you keep at it once or twice a day, your older puppy will learn how to stay. Once that happens, add distractions. Ask someone else to walk across the room or talk to your dog. Or turn on the television or open a door. Rustle some paper that sounds like a treat bag. Be sure that you reward your dog handsomely for resisting temptation.

The last step is to take your *stay* lesson out of the house. Go to a dog park or a pet store and try it. You may have to start back at the beginning in the face of so many distractions, but progress should go much faster.

DOWN

The *down* is related to the sit and should come after your dog knows the *sit* command. Down is useful at mealtimes when you want your dog to lie quietly while you eat, or at any other time when you are conversing with someone and he should quietly wait for you.

Down is another command for which you can choose a word. If you have started saying, "Get down" to your puppy when he jumps on people, you might want to choose another word for the *down*. Or you could switch to "off" when your puppy is jumping on people. Consistency is very important in training a dog; everyone in the family must agree on a word and use it only for one command.

1. Start with your dog sitting in front of you and a highly prized treat such as cooked steak in your hand.

2. Hold the treat in front of your dog's nose and lure him down to the floor. Only give him the treat if his elbows touch the floor.
3. Be sure to say the release word so that he knows he can get up.

WALK NICELY ON LEASH/HEEL

Walking nicely on leash/heeling is the hardest of the basic commands for some Goldens to learn. Energetic, enthusiastic, and curious, your puppy will want to just take off and race to the end of the leash and pull. Puppies are usually raring to go, and walking sedately by your side is not their top priority. But heeling or walking nicely on a leash

Walking nicely on a leash is a very important skill for a big dog like the Golden.

is a very important skill for a big dog such as a Golden. When your puppy is full grown, he will be able to pull amazingly hard at the end of the leash. Goldens are so strong that yours may even pull you down or pull your arm until it is sore, and in the process end up gasping and straining against the collar. This is not a pleasant experience, and people with dogs who do this rarely walk them. The dog is left out of one of dogdom's most pleasant experiences. Even paid dog sitters are reluctant to exercise dogs who pull.

So it is best to teach your puppy to walk nicely on a leash while he is still little. First gather your patience. Then put a wide-band collar on your puppy; narrow ones will cut into his throat. Also, get a 6-foot (2-m) nylon or leather leash that is comfortable in your hands. You can use treats or not. In this lesson, walking is usually a reward in itself.

How to Teach *Walk Nicely on Leash*

1. Start off with your puppy on your left side and both hands on the leash.
2. Talk to him and watch him carefully. As soon as he gets to the end of the leash and pulls, stop. Wait until he stops pulling.
3. With a loose leash, start off again.

4. Every time he pulls, stop. Soon he should learn that if he wants to go forward, he has to stay closer to you. This can take a while and requires resolve on your part not to go forward when he is pulling.

A variation of this is to turn and go in the other direction as soon as your puppy starts pulling on the leash. It can be dizzying but also effective. The key, as in all dog training, is consistency. Do not allow your puppy to get away with pulling; just stop and turn when he does so.

How to Teach *Heel*

Heeling occurs when a dog walks at your knee. His head and shoulders just reach your knee, so most of his body is behind you. Teaching this is easier with treats.

1. When your puppy has the idea that he has to walk closer to you, grab a handful of treats and hold one near your knee.
2. Walk slowly forward and give your puppy the treat when he is walking just behind your knee.
3. Start saying "Heel" when you give him the treat.

Heel is useful when you want to walk on a city sidewalk or you see a wide stroller coming toward you. You and a dog walking at *heel* take up less space.

FINDING A PROFESSIONAL TRAINER

If this is your first Golden puppy, a puppy class is a great idea for you and your dog. Even if this is your second puppy, classes are helpful. A professional trainer can help you perfect your style, and a class setting will help socialize your dog. Trainers teach classes through municipal parks and recreation departments. Others can be found on bulletin boards at vets' offices or in large pet stores. Talk to your vet and breeder. Talk to people you see walking other Goldens. Ask if their trainer uses positive methods and is good with big, enthusiastic dogs.

If you have time, visit a class before you enroll your puppy. Avoid trainers who are loud and yell at the dogs. Also, avoid trainers who rely on negative training methods and equipment.

Classes will require your puppy to sit quietly while the trainer explains a lesson. This by itself is enough reason to register. Your puppy will learn to wait in a room full of other dogs and interesting smells. He will learn to focus on you. In a room full of strange and new things, you will be his source of comfort and strength. Puppy class is his first step toward becoming that perfect Golden you know he can become.

CHAPTER
8

SOLVING PROBLEMS WITH YOUR GOLDEN RETRIEVER

No dog is perfect—not even the Golden Retriever. And the neighbor's grown-up Golden who seems close to perfect didn't start out that way. Puppies and adolescent Goldens explore places they shouldn't, eat things they shouldn't, and test your limits just the way all adolescent humans do. The problem is that Goldens learn so fast that those problem behaviors can become their norm unless they are taught the right way to behave.

Anything your Golden does more than once that bothers or annoys you can become a problem behavior. Of course, some are more urgent problems than others. Chewing furniture is a bigger problem than licking your hands, for example. Some problem behaviors, such as darting out an open door, are downright dangerous. Many problem behaviors stem from your dog just being a Golden Retriever, an athletic sporting canine who needs lots of exercise and attention, in an urbanized world of two-career families.

Each breed comes with its own set of problem behaviors that are twisted offshoots of what the dog was originally expected to do. Goldens usually get into trouble that is related to their soft mouths and their ability to run all day with a hunter. If your Golden doesn't get enough exercise, he will look for other ways to use his tremendous energy and endurance—chewing, digging, even barking. If he doesn't develop a deep relationship with a human, the kind he was meant to have with a hunter, he will also fail to live up to civilized standards. He needs to trust a human and know that the human is in charge. And his soft, extra sensitive mouth needs lots of toys and extra patience on your part as he learns not to grab at people.

Even if you have no plans to show or compete with your dog, you know that you admire the well-behaved Goldens in the show ring or field test. If they can do it, so can yours, especially since show or field Goldens are probably in your dog's pedigree only a few generations

Some problem behaviors may be d[ue] to boredom or a lac[k] of exercise.

back. Beth Johnson, longtime breeder of champion show dogs at Summit Golden Retrievers in Wisconsin, says the secret to a well-behaved Golden is to start early. "You work with them when they are really young, bathing, brushing, sticking to a schedule. Regimen is the most important thing with all dogs, just like children." She recommends taking your puppy to a wide variety of places—noisy, smelly, breezy, and with different surfaces to walk on. "Things don't excite them when they see everything early," she says. And dogs who are not excited listen and behave better.

Dog Tale

When we had our first Golden, I put the change from a pizza delivery on a low table next to the door and served the pizza. When I went back, the $5 bill was gone. She had eaten it!

BARKING

Goldens have an impressive-sounding bark that can startle and even frighten people who don't know your dog. Long ago in Scotland, they hunted without barking, and excessive barking is not a problem in many households with Goldens. But a few Goldens do bark excessively, especially when the doorbell rings or a lawn service shows up next door to mow the grass. They start barking, then whip themselves into a frenzy that is hard to stop.

HOW TO STOP IT

Try to figure out why your dog is barking so much. One reason dogs bark is to get attention, so give up any idea of tethering a barking dog to a stake or a tree. And absolutely do not leave your barking Golden in a fenced yard all day. Left out too long, he'll become bored and lonely and bark, hoping that someone will come or hoping to scare away something that frightens him. Dogs left alone all day frequently need more activity in their lives to keep them engaged and interested. They need to know that someone else is in charge—you—and that they can stand down and relax.

Some dogs bark because they suffer from separation anxiety. If this sounds like your Golden, offer him something challenging to work on when you leave in the morning, such as a peanut butter-filled rubber toy or a frozen treat.

Never reward barking, even inadvertently. If you have a puppy barking in the morning to be let out of the crate, don't open the door until he has been silent for at least several seconds. Timing is very important. If he is barking at something

Excessive barking is not usually a problem with Goldens.

on a walk, talk to him; tell him you see the newspaper blowing across the street and it is no big deal. Keep a matter-of-fact tone and continue walking. If your puppy is barking at something outside the door, go to the door, look out, and say "I see it. Thank you for telling me. You can stop now. It's not a problem."

Some trainers recommend teaching a dog to bark on command. Then the dog can learn a "stop barking" command as well. Like training any command, the words you choose must be the same words everyone in the house uses. If you choose "speak" and "quiet," your dog will be confused if someone else in the house starts shouting "Shut up." Timing, again, is everything in teaching these two commands. Say "Speak!" and knock or ring the doorbell. When your dog barks, reward him. When he pauses and is quiet, say "Quiet! Good dog!" and reward him.

Trainers use deconditioning exercises for serious barkers. For doorbell barkers, for example, they ask someone to ring the doorbell every few minutes while they work with the dog, stopping the barking and rewarding quiet with treats or tennis balls. They teach the dog an alternate behavior that will earn a reward, such as going to a nearby blanket and lying down, quietly, every time the doorbell rings. It may take more than one session for an older, persistent barker.

CHEWING

Golden puppies chew for several reasons: Their mouths hurt from teething, they are genetically programmed to enjoy the feel of something in their mouths, they are curious about what that odd thing on the floor tastes like, and they are bored. When a Golden puppy stops chewing is as individual as his personality. Some hardly chew at all, while some chew until they are 18 months old. However, by the time your Golden is two years old, he should have stopped chewing and be able to look at something new on the floor without picking it up.

HOW TO STOP IT

The first thing to do when you have a new dog is to keep anything valuable off the floor and out of reach. Use gates to keep your puppy in a puppy-proofed part of the house. Start with the kitchen and add one room at a time to his living area. Home offices with electrical cords, paper clips, the computer mouse, calculators, and wastebaskets full of paper might be the last room your puppy gets access to.

Puppies are attracted to anything that smells like you—shoes, socks, and underwear head the list. Every Golden owner has a story about a puppy showing up in front of guests carrying dirty underwear in his mouth. When that happens to you, take the underwear out of your puppy's mouth by gently opening his mouth and offering something like a fleece toy in exchange. If you actually catch him picking up something you don't want him to chew, like an electrical cord, say "Leave it!" Immediately praise him if he resists picking it up and offer him something else to chew.

Keep inappropriate items and anything valuable off the floor and out of reach of your Golden.

If your puppy becomes a problem chewer, ask yourself why. Does he get enough outdoor exercise? After a long walk, puppies are too tired to chew. Does he have several different types of toys to chew? Do you spend enough time with him? Is he having difficulty cutting teeth?

Look in his mouth. If you see anything unusual, make a vet appointment. Offer a teething puppy cold things to chew—frozen dog toys, frozen and knotted wet washcloths (good for a limited time and only

under supervision). Also, puppies need both soft and hard things to carry around and chew. At first, they will put holes in things, but they soon learn to carry things without puncturing them.

If you have a problem chewer, invest in a spray designed to make things taste bad to dogs. Look for these sprays in dog food aisles. Spray furniture legs, door moldings, window cranks, electrical cords, garden hoses—anything your puppy has shown a taste for. These sprays come in different flavors from different manufacturers—if one doesn't work, try another.

If your dog is not a puppy any longer but still chewing, ask yourself why. Does he have separation anxiety? Does he chew only when you are not home? Deconditioning a dog to separation anxiety is a specialty of some trainers. They recommend gathering up your things—keys, briefcase, lunch bag, coat—and then sitting in a chair in the house. After doing this a few times, gather up all of your things and go out the door but only for a few minutes. Gradually lengthen the time you are gone. Go slowly and only lengthen the time you are gone if you are sure that your dog managed the last separation without too much anxiety. Also, consider hiring a dog walker to break up your dog's day and tire him out.

Dogs who chew in times of great stress, such as thunderstorms or fireworks, may need medical treatment and prescription medications—ask your vet for advice.

Again, whenever trying to understand and eliminate a problem behavior in an athletic breed like the Golden, ask yourself how much exercise your dog gets. Increasing his activity may help improve any problem behavior. A 2-mile (3-km) walk every day is a good place to start.

DIGGING

Goldens are not the premier diggers in the dog world. They will dig for a treat that has dropped in the grass. They will occasionally try to dig under the fence if there is something attractive in the yard next door. They will dig in the beach sand to discover the source of a delicious smell. Occasionally, they will dig a pit in the shade so that they can flop in its coolness and chill out. But many adult Goldens go through life without soiling their toenails.

HOW TO STOP IT

If you have a Golden who digs, the easiest and fastest solution is to reduce the time he spends alone outdoors. Go out with him and throw a tennis ball until his tongue is hanging out. Block any spaces under fences where he has started to dig. Use cement patio blocks. If you are replacing a chain-link fence, extend it underground.

If your dog digs pits in the shade to lie in, offer him a small wading pool filled with cool water. Consider buying a canine waterbed that cools dogs and leaving it on a deck or patio. Some dog blankets also have cooling ability. Bigger pet stores and dog catalogs offer both. Or you could resort to an old favorite: the doghouse. Placed in the shade and with good ventilation, it might offer your dog a cooler place that he comes to prefer instead of digging.

If your dog likes to dig in the soft earth in a garden, fence it off. Many times a 2-foot (.5-m) decorative border will be enough to keep a Golden out, especially if you consistently say "Leave it" when your dog looks at the garden. Some Goldens

Your can reduce problem digging by playing outside with your Golden.

obey a fence no matter how short. If not, a 4-foot (1-m) fence is your next choice. Consider raised flowerbeds, hanging pots, and tall planters.

HOUSE SOILING

Goldens are easy to housetrain—with consistency and hard work for a few weeks. They should be housetrained completely by six months, although as puppies they will still need to go out more often than an adult. Many are trained even earlier. An adult Golden should be able to stay in the house for the day without house soiling. They are reliable.

If you already have an older dog, it is even easier to train a new puppy. Puppies are programmed to eliminate in a spot that smells like another dog has already used it, so your older dog has left a scent trail in your yard that a puppy can easily read. If you have no yard and walk your dogs, your puppy will also be attracted to already used spots, even if it isn't the same spot he used yesterday.

Most Goldens are housetrained by the time they are six months old.

But that attraction means that you must clean up any accidents in the house fastidiously. Just because Goldens are easy to train doesn't mean that there will be no accidents. All puppies have accidents in the house, so be prepared. Buy an enzyme cleaner that cleans up the smell as well as the stain. Use it every time. Scrub with old towels to eliminate the smell completely, and bleach the old towels.

HOW TO STOP IT

Troubleshooting house-soiling problems starts with a physical checkup. Does your Golden have a urinary infection or diarrhea that is preventing him from controlling his bladder and bowels? If not, the next thing is to analyze how often you take your dog out, and how closely you are watching for a signal. Housetraining builds on success. Your Golden needs several successful trips outside every day to get the idea that this is where he is supposed to empty his bladder and bowels. Someone has to watch for signals during playtime—circling, sniffing, head down, looking for a spot. A Golden who is doing that in the house should be taken outside immediately, so someone has to be watching.

No matter how old your Golden is, a schedule is required to prevent house soiling. If you have a new rescue several years old or a new puppy only a couple of months old, set up a strict schedule and stick to it. A Golden should eat, sleep, and go out in a routine that varies only slightly from day to day. At first the routine will only cover a few hours—wake up, go out, eat, go out, play, go out, sleep. A puppy will follow that routine several times a day. They almost always need to defecate a short time after eating. You can use that to your advantage, and the schedule should be built around that. Gradually, the sleep and playtimes will get longer and the puppy will be able to hold it longer. An adult Golden will also be able to hold it longer.

Understand that rescue dogs sometimes have a bad week when they first move into their new home. Be willing to work with the dog. Stick to the schedule. Praise him when he goes outside and ignore him when he goes inside, unless you catch him in the act. Then say "No!" and immediately take him outside to the same spot. Leave some feces there so that he understands that this is *the* spot. Be excited and happy when he gets the idea and squats down outside. Offer a treat when he is successful.

Also, think about how much water your dog drinks and when. If he is urinating in the house during the night, consider removing the water dish at 8 p.m. every night. Do not put water in his crate. If you go somewhere later than usual, and your puppy comes home and drinks a bowl of water, be sure to let him out later than usual before bedtime to relieve himself. Or if you go on a long walk in the afternoon and he drinks a lot of water, be sure to let him out an extra time. Puppies need plenty of fresh water, but they do not need to drink it all night or just before they go to bed. They just can't hold all that water.

Avoid shouting at or punishing your dog when he makes a mistake. Most Goldens are very trainable once they understand what you want and are physically able to do it. A two- or three-month-old puppy cannot. Neither can a dog who is not on any schedule.

JUMPING UP

Goldens are athletic, energetic dogs who can easily jump up on people and lick their faces or put their paws on their chest. They can also jump up on the lap of a person sitting in a chair. This is not good behavior generally, and it can be dangerous. The best rule in your house is "four on the floor"—four paws on the floor at all times unless you say it is okay. A 70-pound (31.5-kg) dog who jumps up on a stranger or anyone who comes in your house can startle that person, knock her down, and even break lamps or furniture. And few strangers appreciate dog slobber and dog hair on their clothes.

Jumping up usually starts with a cute puppy standing on his hind legs, leaning on your knee looking for food or attention. Remember that he will grow, and what is cute in a small puppy will not be cute later, when he's much larger.

HOW TO STOP IT

Discourage jumping up right from the beginning. Never reward it with food or attention. Ignore your dog when he jumps up by saying "Off" and turning away. Be consistent.

Goldens are athletic, energetic dogs who can easily jump up on people.

Don't let him jump on you one day and then try to enforce the *off* command another. Be sure that everyone in your house agrees to discourage jumping and uses the word "off." (The word "down" has another meaning to your dog—it's one of his basic obedience cues.)

If you have an older puppy or adult dog who jumps up on people, you can still teach him not to. You need a leash, some treats, and a willing friend. Put the leash on your dog and have your friend go outside and ring the bell. If your dog gets excited and jumps on you, say "Off. Sit." Then turn away and wait until he does so before opening the door. After your friend comes in, if your dog jumps up on her, ask her to turn away as you say "Off. Sit." If your Golden sits, praise him and ask your friend to pet him and reward him with a treat. If he doesn't, hold on to the leash, send your friend back outside, and repeat the exercise. The idea is to teach your dog that good things happen when he sits. This exercise should be repeated in several places, such as the sidewalk, the dog park, and even the vet's office. Strangers in dog places will understand and will be most likely to help you.

Even if you allow your dog to jump up on your lap, you should teach him to wait until you give him the okay. He should approach the chair you are sitting in and sit on the floor, looking at you. If you want him in your lap, give a command that means "jump in my lap," such as "Lap." If you don't want him in your lap, say "No" or "Off" and ignore him. If your dog jumps in your lap unasked, stand up. Be consistent about this too. A dog who is allowed to stay when he invites himself into your space will do so repeatedly.

NIPPING

Well-socialized adult Goldens do not usually nip—also called mouthing—but puppies do. Golden puppies put everything in their sensitive mouths to explore and learn about the world. That can include your fingers, arms, legs, or neck, and they will continue to do it to get attention. Fortunately, puppies grow out of this behavior in a few months. But in the meantime, they have very sharp teeth, and it hurts when they nip.

HOW TO STOP IT

Teaching a puppy not to bite is called bite inhibition. The best way for him to learn this is from his littermates. If he bites them too hard, they'll stop playing with him for a short time. Gradually, he'll learn his own strength and how not to use it when playing. You can work on bite inhibition when you feed your puppy treats. If his teeth touch your hand, say "Ow!" and pull the treat away.

st dogs learn bite inhibition from their littermates.

If you are holding a puppy and he nips your arms and neck, immediately say "Ow!" and put him down and ignore him. Walk away. Turn away. Your tone of voice is very important, so avoid raging anger. The puppy is testing his world and his teeth; he is not trying to hurt you. Act hurt rather than mad. But mostly, just ignore him for a short time, maybe 30 seconds.

Children you meet at the park or on the sidewalk may not know that puppies mouth and may say "He bit me!" Supervise interaction between puppies and children carefully. Suggest to the child before she touches the puppy that puppies like to mouth fingers and skin because they taste good to them.

Socializing your puppy will reduce fear biting in an adult dog. Take your puppy to many places and expose him to many things. As he overcomes his fear of newness, he will be less likely to bite.

FINDING PROFESSIONAL HELP

Training your dog is not something you have to do alone. Obedience classes are good for most Goldens. They thrive on attention and treats. If this is your first dog, or your first big dog, sign up for a beginning obedience class, no matter what age your dog is. If you are having a specific problem, such as jumping up, the instructor will be happy to offer you tips because other dog owners in the class have the same problem. In the class, you will realize that you are not the first owner of a dog who jumps on people or pulls on a leash. The instructor may be able to show you how sending a different signal to your dog will correct his misbehavior in a few weeks. However, success in a class usually requires practice at home. Be consistent in your practice.

If you have chronic canine misbehavior in your house, and if this behavior is causing distress to the people in the house, it might be time to find a behavior specialist. A behaviorist is a dog trainer who solves tough, problem behaviors that frustrate the owner. Sometimes behaviorists will take the dog home with them and work with him without you. Sometimes they have special classes for just a

BE AWARE!

Learn to ignore your Golden. A lot of problem behaviors are attention seeking. Turn your back on your dog when he is misbehaving, fold your arms, and just stand still for several seconds. He can read body language.

le out any physical oblems that might causing a change in vior by taking your Golden to the vet.

few dogs. Sometimes they come to your house and address your issues with your dog on your turf.

Finding the right person is key. This specialist has to be good with dogs, but she also has to be able to explain the solution to you and work with you until you can manage it. The two of you should have the same approach to dogs and dog training. Start by asking your obedience class instructor and your vet if they know any behaviorists. Ask owners of other Goldens or other dogs if they know a super dog trainer they would recommend. Call a nearby vet school. Do a search online at the International Association of Animal Behavior Consultants' (IAABC) website (www.iaabc.org).

When you call potential trainers, ask if they use positive methods (they should), if they will come to your house (flexibility is always a good thing), and what their fee schedule is (some may charge by the hour; others may charge by the visit, and they may specify that a visit is two hours).

A behaviorist works differently from an obedience class that has a set curriculum and covers a broad range of topics. Usually, behaviorists are called in to solve one problem, such as counter surfing or barking at the doorbell. They come into your life and they go after only a short time. One visit may be all that your Golden needs to finally "get it." Or it may take several. It depends on the problem and your dog.

CHAPTER

9

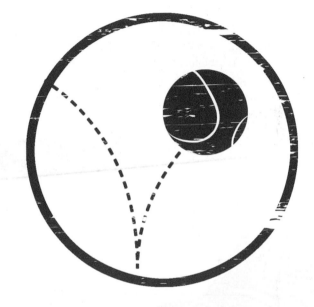

ACTIVITIES
WITH YOUR
GOLDEN RETRIEVER

Think about almost any dog activity you've heard about or seen on television. Somewhere a Golden has tried it and probably succeeded. For example, Goldens have been known to pull a sled—and that versatility is one of their outstanding traits. Goldens can do many things, not just hunt ducks. They can be canine athletes, competing for titles, or social champions, working as therapy dogs. In the world of serious dog competition, Goldens are frequent title winners, and some go on to excel in more than one activity. The first dog to win the new American Kennel Club (AKC) title of Versatile Companion Champion was a Golden Retriever, Jakki, who earned it in 2009 by completing championships in obedience, tracking, and agility.

The Golden is a natural athlete, and because he is so biddable, he can learn to compete in many different ways. He is happiest when he is out somewhere, working alongside you, and he is willing to try anything you suggest. Can every Golden do every activity? No. It's up to you to find your dog's strengths and encourage them by participating in an activity at which he excels. But every healthy Golden can do *something*.

AGILITY

Goldens are naturals at agility, and many have proved it with champion titles. Begun in 1994 by the AKC, the sport pits owner and dog against the clock on a

Goldens are natu
at agility.

course that involves hurdles, weave poles, tunnels, and tall things to climb over. Dogs must be 15 months old to compete, but Goldens should not do any serious jumping before growth plates in the long bones close, which could be as late as 18 months. Be careful with puppies younger than two years old, and go slowly.

Agility is a team sport. Your dog has to run through the tunnel, and you have to direct him from obstacle to obstacle in the designated order. But agility has another level in addition to competition. Many people and dogs who never finish with the top times can learn agility and have fun. Some dog trainers say that agility training—just taking the classes and learning to tackle the obstacles— can be good for timid dogs or rescue dogs who have had a hard start in life. As they learn new things and conquer their fears, without ever setting foot in a competitive ring, these dogs become more confident in everyday life. It is also good for bored dogs who need more activity in their day.

Agility requires equipment that can be purchased or built. Some dog owners find an agility club they can join that allows them to practice with the club's equipment.

CANINE GOOD CITIZEN® TEST

The AKC offers a Canine Good Citizen (CGC) program, which is designed to recognize well-behaved dogs. Dogs who pass a ten-point test earn the designation "Canine Good Citizen" and are entitled to use the initials "CGC" after their name. Many obedience instructors offer a class that teaches all ten behaviors for dogs who have already passed a beginning obedience class. Taking the class and meeting other dog owners who are trying to pass the test, as well as practicing at home, can be a good way for you and your dog to have fun together.

If you fail the first time you take the test, practice and take the test again. Some of the behaviors are easy for Goldens, but not all pass the first time. The test calls for the kind of restraint and manners that a dog only acquires through practice, and some Goldens only acquire these traits after they are two years old.

The ten tested behaviors are accepting a friendly stranger, sitting politely for petting, grooming, walking on a loose lead, walking through a crowd, commands (*sit*, *down*, and *stay*), coming when called, politely walking by another dog, reacting acceptably to a distraction such as a loud noise or wheelchair, and not panicking when you leave him in a room with other people.

CONFORMATION

The Golden who shows in conformation is a joy to behold: trim, well groomed, and apt to strike a majestic pose. Goldens should be shown in top physical condition, able to run all day and hunt birds if asked. Most show

Goldens who com in conformation should be in top physical conditio

dogs are bred by specialized breeders and selected as puppies for a career in the show ring, instead of a life as a companion. If you have such a dog and want to try the conformation ring, you're in for a roller coaster ride full of heady excitement mixed with some disappointment. Be prepared to win one day and lose the next.

Work with your breeder until you learn how dog shows operate. Judges reward dogs who match the Golden Retriever standard and have that indefinable special something. In the end, it is a judgment call. Judges look for correct gait, teeth, eyes, ears, topline, coat, and bone, among many other things. Show dogs must not be spayed or neutered, so hold off on that surgery until your dog has a chance to prove herself or himself in the ring.

Look for an obedience club near you that offers conformation or handler classes so that you can learn the secrets of making your dog look his best. If your dog proves to be a serious winner, consider hiring a professional handler for AKC shows. The United Kennel Club (UKC) also runs dog shows, but it does not allow professional handlers. Because all show dogs are handled by owners, a UKC show may be a good place for you and your puppy to start in conformation. Puppies as young as six months can be shown in the conformation ring.

If you want to show your puppy, teach him to stand right from the beginning. Make it a game and keep training sessions short—a few seconds at first, a few minutes at most. You can see how well your dog matches the show standard at www.akc.org, www.ukcdogs.com, and www.grca.org. Dogs must be registered with the chosen organization to be eligible for show entry.

FIELD TESTS

Golden Retrievers are eligible to compete in AKC retriever field tests, known to be a difficult test of a dog's hunting ability. The dog is sent to retrieve a bird up to 250 or 300 yards (228.5 or 274.5 m) away, over land and water. The dog must not be afraid of water, gunshots, or birds, and he must be excellent at off-leash obedience. He must be able to wait with the hunter until he is instructed to get the bird. Dead birds are thrown up in the air and sometimes the dog is allowed to watch and mark where the bird fell. Other times, he is not allowed to watch and must find the bird by following instructions from his hunter.

Field trial dogs must be in top physical condition, extremely well trained, and have an ability to retrieve a bird and return it to the owner without damaging it. Start with a young dog, find a field dog club, and consider getting professional help from a trainer if this sport interests you.

Golden is adept retrieving in water, you may want to consider field tests.

HUNT TESTS

Golden Retrievers are first and always hunting dogs. The hunt test challenges their abilities in a field, hunting and retrieving downed birds, and attempts to recreate a true hunting situation. Dogs who retrieve well can earn hunting titles: Junior Hunter (JH), Senior Hunter (SH), and Master Hunter (MH). Dogs are judged against a standard—not against each other—so many dogs may pass a hunt test.

Live birds are shot while dogs wait at a starting line. They are then commanded to retrieve the birds. A Golden might have to go through water, carry a dead or injured bird, and return with the bird to his hunter without damaging it. He may also have to retrieve a bird he did not see fall by following instructions from his hunter.

Goldens in hunt tests must be in top physical condition, accept the sound of guns, be able to retrieve across land and water, and carry a bird without damaging it. Hunt tests are sometimes considered more realistic than field tests, and may be a better place for beginners to start. Find a retriever field club, which will have experienced hunters who can help you.

OBEDIENCE

Competitive obedience is the art of precision. Many Goldens excel at it; more Goldens get obedience titles than any other breed, and many more Goldens get

Hunt tests chall[e]
a dog's ability t[o]
hunt and retriev[e]
downed birds.

Obedience is a team sport that requires a lot of precision.

obedience titles than conformation titles. Obedience is a team sport—dog and handler work as one to accomplish a series of exercises in front of a judge. The exercises are at three levels—Novice, Open, and Utility—and involve heeling, jumping hurdles, retrieving dumbbells, staying in place, coming when called, and picking out a dumbbell that the owner handled. Dogs who accomplish the requirements at the Novice level earn a Companion Dog title; at the Open level they earn a Companion Dog Excellent; and at the Utility level they can earn both a Utility Dog and a Utility Dog Excellent title.

Obedience always has some level of uncertainty. Even well-trained dogs will be distracted some days and wander off when they are supposed to be sitting. But people who do well at obedience stick to it, practice at home, take classes that provide distractions to teach the dog how to ignore them, and understand that their dog is a living, breathing animal, not a machine.

Start with basic obedience classes when your dog is a puppy and keep at it. Make it fun. Focus is very important in an obedience dog, so teach your puppy the *watch me* command:

1. Hold food in both hands in front of your face.
2. Move your hands away from your face out past your shoulders.
3. When your puppy gives up looking at one piece of food or the other and

looks at you, say "Watch me!" and give him the food. Or use a squeak a toy or a clicker, and when he looks at you, say "Watch me!" and offer him a treat.

Some breeders breed dogs specifically for obedience and other activities, not the show ring, so if you are looking for a puppy and are interested in obedience, ask to see obedience titles in his pedigree. Dogs who compete in obedience, whether in the AKC or UKC, must be registered.

RALLY

A good introduction to canine competition may be rally, a dog sport created for pet owners that the AKC began sponsoring in 2005. It is designed for beginners but works best with a dog who has some obedience training, such as for the CGC program. Your dog must be on a leash (a loose leash), and you are allowed to talk to him, unlike in competitive obedience. The two of you work as a team, proceeding through a course with 10 to 20 stations. At each station, a sign tells your dog to do several things, such as jump, change pace, and come to the front of you. AKC rally has three levels—Novice, Advanced, and Excellent—each one more challenging than the previous. By the third level, a dog must back up three steps and stand while the owner walks completely around him.

Because you need a course with signs that tell you what to do at each station, and a dog who will cooperate in a very distracting environment, it is best to prepare for rally with a dog trainer who teaches a rally class.

The Golden's fri
personality mal
a great therapy

THERAPY WORK

Many Goldens make great therapy dogs. A therapy dog is not a service dog, permanently assigned to do things for an individual who can't do them for herself, such as a dog from Leader Dogs for the Blind. Therapy dogs work alongside their owners a few days a month, bringing comfort and love to people in hospitals and nursing homes. They listen to children read at public libraries, and they visit trauma sites and comfort people who have been through a disaster.

If you want your Golden to be a therapy dog, he must be certified by a therapy dog organization such as Therapy Dogs International (TDI) (www.tdi-dog.org) or the Delta Society (www.deltasociety.org). Sometimes therapy organizations require a CGC certificate, plus an additional test that may include walking sedately past treats thrown on the ground. They test the handler and the dog together. Taking a large dog into a small hospital room filled with wires requires skill on the handler's part and a well-behaved dog who doesn't pull on the leash.

Therapy dogs engage in different types of work, so you can match your dog's personality to the job. But all therapy dogs should like people, be willing to let strangers touch them, and be tolerant of minor mishaps such as someone leaning on them, stepping on their foot, or even pulling their hair by mistake. Exceptional therapy dogs have a sixth sense for people who need their attention and will offer love without being coached.

TRACKING

In tracking, unlike in any other canine sport, the dog is in charge. A trained tracking dog in harness follows a scent through a field, his owner trailing behind at the end of a long lead. Goldens, hunting dogs who found downed birds in Scotland, can be exceptional trackers, but it takes patience to train them to follow the right scent. Most people in tracking have stories about how their dog was following the track until it crossed a deer track, and the dog abandoned the "right" track and veered off on the deer track.

It is best to learn tracking from experienced trackers out in the field. Dogs must be taught to follow a track freshly laid by someone who's not the owner, and laying a track is a skill in itself. The tracklayer walks a path, mapping the direction she went and leaving her scent and an item at the end of the trail, such as a glove. The dog is then offered something she wore, such as a bandanna, and asked to find the trail and the glove. Three levels of competition—tracking dog, tracking dog excellent, and variable surface tracking—involve courses of varying lengths up to 1,000 yards (914.5 m) with up to eight turns. In tracking competition the clock is not important, and dogs must be on a lead at all times.

Tracking is for independent-thinking dogs, owners who like to be outdoors in all weather, and dogs and owners who like to do things together with a group of dog lovers. If this sounds like fun to you, find a dog obedience club or field dog club and ask about tracking classes.

TRAVEL

If you get involved in serious dog activities, you may be traveling with your dog to events in other cities or even other states. Moving your household from one city to another will also require a trip with your dog. And if you plan a vacation carefully, you can travel with your dog just for fun.

Traveling with your Golden Retriever is very doable. It requires planning and anticipation of your dog's needs—food, water, exercise, safety, and time with you. But if you think it through ahead of time, you and your dog can have a fun trip.

TRAVEL BY CAR

Most Goldens love going in the car, and learn "car" as one of their first and favorite words. They jump eagerly into the car, enjoy being in it, and look out the window or curl up and sleep to the rhythm of the engine. Goldens can travel in raised crates so that they can look out the window, or they can sit in a rear seat, securely attached to a seatbelt with a dog harness designed for cars. (Goldens should never ride in front because of the danger that air bags present when they inflate.)

When traveling by car, pack for your Golden as carefully as if he were a person. Take enough water from home for the day; food, water, and food dishes; poop bags; leashes; treats; toys; old towels; and something soft the dog can mouth in the car, like a fleece toy. If you are going to be staying somewhere overnight, take copies of your dog's vaccination records with you and a blanket or traveling bed for him to sleep on. Also pack a first-aid kit and keep it in the car: tweezers, bandages, flashlight, antibiotic ointment, shampoo—anything you think you might need if your Golden gets hurt or into something he shouldn't. Include your vet's phone number and the number of a poison center. Be sure that your Golden has an ID tag on his collar with a cell phone number so that someone can reach you if he slips out at a rest stop or parking lot. Keep the windows up far enough so that he cannot jump out or put his head out; flying debris can damage his eyes. Be prepared to stop every couple of hours and let your dog walk around outside, always on leash. If you are taking a long road trip, try to get a real walk in halfway through.

Occasionally, a Golden will get carsick—with drooling, nausea, even vomiting or diarrhea, and definitely unhappiness. If this sounds like your dog, try acclimating him to the car with short trips only at first, building up to longer rides. Also, try gingersnaps to settle his stomach, or try withholding food for several hours before you go in the car. Talk to your vet, and hope that your carsick dog grows out of it.

TRAVEL BY AIR

When traveling by air, a few adult Goldens, such as service dogs, can ride in the cabin, but due to their size, most will have to fly in a crate in the cargo area. Show dogs fly this way frequently, but for the average pet, flying is stressful. If you have to fly with your dog, try to book a nonstop flight to avoid the delays of a connection. Check with the airline on crate requirements (for example, heavy plastic crates only, large labels saying "LIVE ANIMAL"), and be sure that your dog can sit up in the crate and stand and turn around. Most likely, the airline will require a vet to sign a health certificate within ten days of your flight.

With careful anning, you can your Golden on ation with you.

Take copies of vaccination records with you. Line the crate with an absorbent paper or fabric pad. Include a soft toy for your pet. If you have a very long flight day, consider taping a small bag of food to the crate for the crew to feed your dog. This will not work with all dogs, and just the opposite may be better—some dogs fly better on an empty stomach. Some experienced travelers recommend securely attaching a small water dish to the crate and filling it with ice—preferably a block of ice you froze ahead of time—so that it stays cold throughout the flight.

Be sure that your dog is wearing an ID tag with your name and phone number. The crate should also be clearly marked with both your home address and the crate's destination on this flight. Sedating a dog about to fly is often considered a bad idea because no one can check on him to see how he is reacting to the sedative and altitude change. Check with your vet and airline.

A new airline, Pet Airways (petairways.com), started transporting pets in 2009 in the cabin of a converted airplane to a limited number of US cities. Pets fly in crates in the cabin, along with an attendant who keeps an eye on them.

PET-FRIENDLY LODGING

So you want your dog to go with the family on a summer vacation to the lake? The good news is that more hotels accept dogs. The sobering news is that this idyllic vacation will take extra work and cost a little more. But if you are willing to plan ahead, it can be a great adventure.

The first thing to realize is that smuggling a dog like a Golden Retriever into a motel is almost impossible. You need a reservation. Plot your trip, pick likely spots for overnight stays, and start calling motels, asking "Do you allow dogs in the rooms?" Ask if there is a pet fee. If you need to rent a cottage, do the same thing. Start early. Although more hotels than ever are pet friendly, sometimes they have only two or three rooms set aside for pets. If you have a choice, opt for a first-floor room to avoid elevators or stairs.

BE AWARE!

At some point, dogs cross a threshold and shut down. It can happen to Goldens who have been overrehearsed, expected to do too much in one day, or stressed by noise. Watch your dog carefully in any activity and know when to stop for the day.

all local laws and or motel rules for and fun getaway with your Golden.

Be sure to pack poop bags and pick up after your dog. Whether the motel stays pet-friendly may depend on you. Many motels will ask that you not leave the dog alone in the room or that you leave the dog only if he is crated. They are trying to prevent canine anxiety attacks that may result in frenzied barking or chewing. Some Goldens will be happy wherever you are, plopping down and sleeping through the night. Others will miss their own home, at least the first night, pacing a little and checking in with you more than usual. If you have a dog like this, set up a dog bed right next to your bed so that he can be as close to you as he wants. Be understanding but matter of fact, and don't encourage his worries by coddling him.

Take food and water, bowls, shampoo and old towels, treats, and chew toys. Try to stick to the meal schedule your dog is used to, and discourage treats that strangers offer him, like the ends of hot dog buns or corn chips.

RESOURCES

ASSOCIATIONS AND ORGANIZATIONS

BREED CLUBS

American Kennel Club (AKC)
5580 Centerview Drive
Raleigh, NC 27606
Telephone: (919) 233-9767
Fax: (919) 233-3627
E-Mail: info@akc.org
www.akc.org

Canadian Kennel Club (CKC)
89 Skyway Avenue, Suite 100
Etobicoke, Ontario M9W 6R4
Telephone: (416) 675-5511
Fax: (416) 675-6506
E-Mail: information@ckc.ca
www.ckc.ca

Federation Cynologique Internationale (FCI)
Secretariat General de la FCI
Place Albert 1er, 13
B – 6530 Thuin
Belqique
www.fci.be

The Golden Retriever Club (GRC)
www.thegoldenretrieverclub.co.uk

Golden Retriever Club of America (GRCA)
www.grca.org

The Kennel Club
1 Clarges Street
London
W1J 8AB
Telephone: 0870 606 6750
Fax: 0207 518 1058
www.the-kennel-club.org.uk

United Kennel Club (UKC)
100 E. Kilgore Road
Kalamazoo, MI 49002-5584
Telephone: (269) 343-9020
Fax: (269) 343-7037
E-Mail: pbickell@ukcdogs.com
www.ukcdogs.com

PET SITTERS

National Association of Professional Pet Sitters
15000 Commerce Parkway, Suite C
Mt. Laurel, New Jersey 08054
Telephone: (856) 439-0324
Fax: (856) 439-0525
E-Mail: napps@ahint.com
www.petsitters.org

Pet Sitters International
201 East King Street
King, NC 27021-9161
Telephone: (336) 983-9222
Fax: (336) 983-5266
E-Mail: info@petsit.com
www.petsit.com

RESCUE ORGANIZATIONS AND ANIMAL WELFARE GROUPS

American Humane Association (AHA)
63 Inverness Drive East
Englewood, CO 80112
Telephone: (303) 792-9900
Fax: 792-5333
www.americanhumane.org

American Society for the Prevention of Cruelty to Animals (ASPCA)
424 E. 92nd Street
New York, NY 10128-6804
Telephone: (212) 876-7700
www.aspca.org

The Humane Society of the United States (HSUS)
2100 L Street, NW
Washington DC 20037
Telephone: (202) 452-1100
www.hsus.org

Royal Society for the Prevention of Cruelty to Animals (RSPCA)
RSPCA Enquiries Service
Wilberforce Way, Southwater,
Horsham, West Sussex RH13 9RS
United Kingdom
Telephone: 0870 3335 999
Fax: 0870 7530 284
www.rspca.org.uk

SPORTS

International Agility Link (IAL)
Global Administrator: Steve Drinkwater
E-Mail: yunde@powerup.au
www.agilityclick.com/~ial

The World Canine Freestyle Organization, Inc.
P.O. Box 350122
Brooklyn, NY 11235
Telephone: (718) 332-8336
Fax: (718) 646-2686
E-Mail: WCFODOGS@aol.com
www.worldcaninefreestyle.org

THERAPY

Delta Society
875 124th Ave, NE, Suite 101
Bellevue, WA 98005
Telephone: (425) 679-5500
Fax: (425) 679-5539
E-Mail: info@DeltaSociety.org
www.deltasociety.org

erapy Dogs Inc.
). Box 20227
eyenne WY 82003
lephone: (877) 843-7364
c: (307) 638-2079
Mail: therapydogsinc@
estoffice.net
vw.therapydogs.com

erapy Dogs International (TDI)
Bartley Road
nders, NJ 07836
ephone: (973) 252-9800
: (973) 252-7171
Mail: tdi@gti.net
w.tdi-dog.org

AINING

ociation of Pet Dog Trainers
OT)
North Main Street, Suite 610
enville, SC 29601
phone: 1-800) PET-DOGS
(864) 331-0767
ail: information@apdt.com
w.apdt.com

rnational Association of
nal Behavior Consultants
BC)
Callery Road
berry Township, PA 16066
ail: info@iaabc.org
v.iaabc.org

onal Association of Dog
dience Instructors (NADOI)
369
Grapevine Hwy.
t, TX 76054-2085
.nadoi.org

VETERINARY AND HEALTH RESOURCES

Academy of Veterinary Homeopathy (AVH)
P.O. Box 9280
Wilmington, DE 19809
Telephone: (866) 652-1590
Fax: (866) 652-1590
www.theavh.org

American Academy of Veterinary Acupuncture (AAVA)
P.O. Box 1058
Glastonbury, CT 06033
Telephone: (860) 632-9911
Fax: (860) 659-8772
www.aava.org

American Animal Hospital Association (AAHA)
12575 W. Bayaud Ave.
Lakewood, CO 80228
Telephone: (303) 986-2800
Fax: (303) 986-1700
E-Mail: info@aahanet.org
www.aahanet.org/index.cfm

American College of Veterinary Internal Medicine (ACVIM)
1997 Wadsworth Blvd., Suite A
Lakewood, CO 80214-5293
Telephone: (800) 245-9081
Fax: (303) 231-0880
Email: ACVIM@ACVIM.org
www.acvim.org

American College of Veterinary Ophthalmologists (ACVO)
P.O. Box 1311
Meridian, ID 83860
Telephone: (208) 466-7624
Fax: (208) 466-7693
E-Mail: office09@acvo.com
www.acvo.com

American Holistic Veterinary Medical Association (AHVMA)
2218 Old Emmorton Road
Bel Air, MD 21015
Telephone: (410) 569-0795
Fax: (410) 569-2346
E-Mail: office@ahvma.org
www.ahvma.org

American Veterinary Medical Association (AVMA)
1931 North Meacham Road, Suite 100
Schaumburg, IL 60173-4360
Telephone: (847) 925-8070
Fax: (847) 925-1329
E-Mail: avmainfo@avma.org
www.avma.org

ASPCA Animal Poison Control Center
Telephone: (888) 426-4435
www.aspca.org

British Veterinary Association (BVA)
7 Mansfield Street
London
W1G 9NQ
Telephone: 0207 636 6541
Fax: 0207 908 6349
E-Mail: bvahq@bva.co.uk
www.bva.co.uk

Canine Eye Registration Foundation (CERF)
VMDB/CERF
1717 Philo Rd
P O Box 3007
Urbana, IL 61803-3007
Telephone: (217) 693-4800
Fax: (217) 693-4801
E-Mail: CERF@vmbd.org
www.vmdb.org

Orthopedic Foundation for
Animals (OFA)
2300 NE Nifong Blvd
Columbus, Missouri 65201-3856
Telephone: (573) 442-0418
Fax: (573) 875-5073
Email: ofa@offa.org
www.offa.org

US Food and Drug Administration
Center for Veterinary Medicine
(CVM)
7519 Standish Place
HFV-12
Rockville, MD 20855-0001
Telephone: (240) 276-9300 or (888)
INFO-FDA
http://www.fda.gov/cvm

PUBLICATIONS
BOOKS

Adamson, Eve. Terra-Nova *The
Golden Retriever*. Neptune City:
TFH Publications, Inc.,
2005.

Anderson, Teoti. *The Super Simple
Guide to Housetraining*. Neptune
City: TFH Publications, 2004.

Anne, Jonna, with Mary Straus.
*The Healthy Dog Cookbook: 50
Nutritious and Delicious
Recipes Your Dog Will Love*. UK: Ivy
Press Limited, 2008.

Boneham, Sheila Webster, Ph.D.
Animal Planet *Golden Retrievers*.
Neptune City: TFH
Publications, Inc., 2006.

Dainty, Suellen. *50 Games to Play
With Your Dog*. UK: Ivy Press
Limited, 2007.

McCullough, Susan. DogLife *Golden
Retriever*. Neptune City: TFH
Publications, Inc., 2010.

MAGAZINES
AKC Family Dog
American Kennel Club
260 Madison Avenue
New York, NY 10016
Telephone: (800) 490-5675
E-Mail: familydog@akc.org
www.akc.org/pubs/familydog

AKC Gazette
American Kennel Club
260 Madison Avenue
New York, NY 10016
Telephone: (800) 533-7323
E-Mail: gazette@akc.org
www.akc.org/pubs/gazette

Dog & Kennel
Pet Publishing, Inc.
7-L Dundas Circle
Greensboro, NC 27407
Telephone: (336) 292-4272
Fax: (336) 292-4272
E-Mail: info@petpublishing.com
www.dogandkennel.com

Dogs Monthly
Ascot House
High Street, Ascot,
Berkshire SL5 7JG
United Kingdom
Telephone: 0870 730 8433
Fax: 0870 730 8431
E-Mail: admin@rtc-associates.
freeserve.co.uk
www.corsini.co.uk/dogsmonthly

WEBSITES
Nylabone
www.nylabone.com

TFH Publications, Inc.
www.tfh.com

PHOTO CREDITS

DEDICATION

To the five Goldens who shared their lives with me (Bailey, Mac, Dash, Scout, and Ben) and taught me how much this sweet breed offers.

ACKNOWLEDGMENTS

Thanks to Marcia Schlehr, Amy Booth, and Rhonda Hovan, Golden Retriever experts who generously helped me. Thanks to Charlotte Reed, pet writing expert who introduced me to all the right people. Thanks to Stephanie Fornino and Heather Russell-Revesz, editing experts at TFH who made my words better. And, as always, thanks to Tom, for everything.

ABOUT THE AUTHOR

Sheila O'Brien Schimpf is a prize-winning journalist who lives in East Lansing, Michigan, with three Golden Retrievers. One of her Goldens was a breeding stock dog who whelped 20 puppies in Sheila's kitchen for a service dog agency. Sheila has written for *The Lansing State Journal*, BNA.com, and *Dog Fancy* magazine and is the author of DogLife *Yorkshire Terrier*. Occasionally, she teaches journalism at Michigan State University. She is married and has three grown children.

ABOUT ANIMAL PLANET™

Animal Planet™ is the only television network dedicated exclusively to the connection between humans and animals. The network brings people of all ages together by tapping into our fundamental fascination with animals through an array of fresh programming that includes humor, competition, drama, and spectacle from the animal kingdom.

ABOUT *DOGS 101*

The most comprehensive—and most endearing—dog encyclopedia on television, *DOGS 101* spotlights the adorable, the feisty and the unexpected. A wide-ranging rundown of everyone's favorite dog breeds—from the Dalmatian to Xoloitzcuintli—this series surveys a variety of breeds for their behavioral quirks, genetic history, most famous examples and wildest trivia. Learn which dogs are best for urban living and which would be the best fit for your family. Using a mix of animal experts, pop-culture footage and stylized dog photography, *DOGS 101* is an unprecedented look at man's best friend.